READINGS ON

GREAT
EXPECTATIONS

OTHER TITLES IN THE GREENHAVEN PRESS LITERARY COMPANION SERIES:

AMERICAN AUTHORS

Maya Angelou
Stephen Crane
Emily Dickinson
William Faulkner
F. Scott Fitzgerald
Nathaniel Hawthorne
Ernest Hemingway
Herman Melville
Arthur Miller
Eugene O'Neill
Edgar Allan Poe
John Steinbeck
Mark Twain
Thornton Wilder

AMERICAN LITERATURE

The Adventures of
  Huckleberry Finn
The Adventures of Tom
  Sawyer
The Catcher in the Rye
The Crucible
Death of a Salesman
The Glass Menagerie
The Grapes of Wrath
The Great Gatsby
Of Mice and Men
The Old Man and the Sea
The Pearl
The Scarlet Letter
A Separate Peace

BRITISH AUTHORS

Jane Austen
Joseph Conrad
Charles Dickens

BRITISH LITERATURE

Animal Farm
The Canterbury Tales
Hamlet
Julius Caesar
Lord of the Flies
Macbeth
Pride and Prejudice
Romeo and Juliet
Shakespeare: The Comedies
Shakespeare: The Histories
Shakespeare: The Sonnets
Shakespeare: The Tragedies
A Tale of Two Cities
Wuthering Heights

WORLD AUTHORS

Fyodor Dostoyevsky
Homer
Sophocles

WORLD LITERATURE

All Quiet on the Western
  Front
The Diary of a Young Girl
A Doll's House

THE GREENHAVEN PRESS
Literary Companion
TO BRITISH LITERATURE

READINGS ON

GREAT EXPECTATIONS

David L. Bender, *Publisher*
Bruno Leone, *Executive Editor*
Bonnie Szumski, *Series Editor*
Lawrence Kappel, *Book Editor*

Greenhaven Press, San Diego, CA

1657 4210
L

Every effort has been made to trace the owners of copy-righted material. The articles in this volume may have been edited for content, length, and/or reading level. The titles have been changed to enhance the editorial purpose. Those interested in locating the original source will find the complete citation on the first page of each article.

Library of Congress Cataloging-in-Publication Data

Readings on Great expectations / Lawrence Kappel, book editor.
        p.   cm. — (The Greenhaven Press literary companion to British literature)
    Includes bibliographical references and index.
    ISBN 1-56510-821-3 (lib. bdg. : alk. paper). —
ISBN 1-56510-820-5 (pbk. : alk. paper)
    1. Dickens, Charles, 1812–1870. Great expectations. 2. Young men in literature. 3. Bildungsroman.   I. Kappel, Lawrence.
II. Series.
PR4560.R43   1999
823'.8—dc21   98-24128
                                                      CIP

Cover photo: Culver Pictures
Library of Congress, 15, 16, 24, 26

Copyright ©1999 by Greenhaven Press, Inc.
PO Box 289009
San Diego, CA 92198-9009
Printed in the U.S.A.

"Such a very fine, new, and grotesque idea has opened upon me, that I . . . reserve the notion for a new book. . . . It so opens out before me *that I can see the whole of a serial revolving on it, in a most singular and comic manner.* **"**

Charles Dickens, on his first inspiration for Great Expectations

CONTENTS

Chapter 1: Major Themes in *Great Expectations*

Chapter 2: Symbols and Structure in *Great Expectations*

FOREWORD

*"'Tis the good reader that
makes the good book."*

Ralph Waldo Emerson

The story's bare facts are simple: The captain, an old and scarred seafarer, walks with a peg leg made of whale ivory. He relentlessly drives his crew to hunt the world's oceans for the great white whale that crippled him. After a long search, the ship encounters the whale and a fierce battle ensues. Finally the captain drives his harpoon into the whale, but the harpoon line catches the captain about the neck and drags him to his death.

A simple story, a straightforward plot—yet, since the 1851 publication of Herman Melville's *Moby-Dick*, readers and critics have found many meanings in the struggle between Captain Ahab and the whale. To some, the novel is a cautionary tale that depicts how Ahab's obsession with revenge leads to his insanity and death. Others believe that the whale represents the unknowable secrets of the universe and that Ahab is a tragic hero who dares to challenge fate by attempting to discover this knowledge. Perhaps Melville intended Ahab as a criticism of Americans' tendency to become involved in well-intentioned but irrational causes. Or did Melville model Ahab after himself, letting his fictional character express his anger at what he perceived as a cruel and distant god?

Although literary critics disagree over the meaning of *Moby-Dick*, readers do not need to choose one particular interpretation in order to gain an understanding of Melville's

9

novel. Instead, by examining various analyses, they can gain numerous insights into the issues that lie under the surface of the basic plot. Studying the writings of literary critics can also aid readers in making their own assessments of *Moby-Dick* and other literary works and in developing analytical thinking skills.

The Greenhaven Literary Companion Series was created with these goals in mind. Designed for young adults, this unique anthology series provides an engaging and comprehensive introduction to literary analysis and criticism. The essays included in the Literary Companion Series are chosen for their accessibility to a young adult audience and are expertly edited in consideration of both the reading and comprehension levels of this audience. In addition, each essay is introduced by a concise summation that presents the contributing writer's main themes and insights. Every anthology in the Literary Companion Series contains a varied selection of critical essays that cover a wide time span and express diverse views. Wherever possible, primary sources are represented through excerpts from authors' notebooks, letters, and journals and through contemporary criticism.

Each title in the Literary Companion Series pays careful consideration to the historical context of the particular author or literary work. In-depth biographies and detailed chronologies reveal important aspects of authors' lives and emphasize the historical events and social milieu that influenced their writings. To facilitate further research, every anthology includes primary and secondary source bibliographies of articles and/or books selected for their suitability for young adults. These engaging features make the Greenhaven Literary Companion series ideal for introducing students to literary analysis in the classroom or as a library resource for young adults researching the world's great authors and literature.

Exceptional in its focus on young adults, the Greenhaven Literary Companion Series strives to present literary criticism in a compelling and accessible format. Every title in the series is intended to spark readers' interest in leading American and world authors, to help them broaden their understanding of literature, and to encourage them to formulate their own analyses of the literary works that they read. It is the editors' hope that young adult readers will find these anthologies to be true companions in their study of literature.

INTRODUCTION

The English novelist Charles Dickens has been a favorite author throughout much of the world for over a hundred years. Most people know Dickens through Ebenezer Scrooge of "A Christmas Carol" or the innocent boy in the criminal world of *Oliver Twist*. Many know his drama of the guillotine and the French Revolution, *A Tale of Two Cities*. But few literary critics and scholars consider these his best works; most cite instead the less famous Dickens novels *Bleak House, Little Dorrit*, and *Our Mutual Friend*.

Great Expectations, however, is one Dickens novel that stands out from the rest in being loved and admired by both ordinary readers and the experts. For the skill and artistry of its story-telling and character development, and for the depth of its insight into human experience, it is widely considered the very best of Dickens's fifteen novels. It has been made into five popular film versions—in 1934, 1947, 1974, 1989, and 1998. As eminent Dickens critic J. Hillis Miller has said:

> *Great Expectations* is the most unified and concentrated expression of Dickens' abiding sense of the world, and Pip might be called the archetypal Dickens hero. In *Great Expectations* Dickens' particular view of things is expressed with a concreteness and symbolic intensity he never surpassed.

The story is full of action and emotion, mystery and suspense. Published first in weekly installments over an eight-month period in 1860–1861, *Great Expectations* unfolds through a skillfully managed plot that engages the first-time modern reader's immediate attention just as it did for those original readers who waited for each weekly installment. But it is its rich treatment of universal themes that is most responsible for the power of *Great Expectations* and that keeps readers coming back to it, generation after generation. And the character of Pip remains intriguing as he grows and changes throughout the course of the novel.

Such a "novel of education," with a quest for identity at its heart, clearly has social, psychological, and moral dimensions, and it is possible to view the novel from each of these three perspectives. Some readers respond primarily to the novel's social themes, such as class and snobbery; others have focused their attention on the psychological themes, such as guilt and shame; and a third group has been concerned with the moral meaning of the novel. The essays selected for this Greenhaven Literary Companion to Charles Dickens's *Great Expectations* reflect a variety of interpretations from each of the three perspectives, as well as overviews of the novel's plot, characters, and structure.

Each of the essays is introduced by a guide to its key points, which are further identified within the essays through subheadings. As a further aid to understanding, inserts within selected essays illuminate important ideas and add supplemental information. An annotated table of contents offers brief previews of the individual essays, and a chronology of key dates in Dickens's life and career provides historical context. Further reading on Dickens and *Great Expectations* is indicated, and research is facilitated by a bibliography carefully selected for young adults. A biographical introduction, while reviewing Dickens's life and career, focuses on issues in his experience that are relevant to *Great Expectations*. These tools and the essays themselves provide the basis of an enhanced and enriched reading of this classic novel.

DICKENS'S LIFE AND GREAT EXPECTATIONS

The American and French Revolutions had occurred only twenty or thirty years before Charles Dickens was born, and the ideal of liberation from oppressive government and corrupt societies was still vital and new when he was growing up. This spirit informs all of Dickens's novels. But there was no revolution in England, so injustice and social problems had to be dealt with through reform, through legislation within the system, and perhaps most important, through public awareness. Dickens's works did much to educate people on the social conditions of his day.

In Dickens's native England, Queen Victoria was in the twenty-fourth year of her reign when *Great Expectations* was published, having ascended to the throne while Dickens was publishing his first novel, *Pickwick Papers,* in 1837 (she would remain the queen of England for the rest of the nineteenth century). During her remarkable reign—and during Dickens's reign as the country's foremost writer—England became the most powerful and wealthy nation in the world, as the United States would become in the twentieth century.

To be a great culture, Victorian England needed creativity and beauty, and a moral conscience as well as worldly success. As the most influential novelist of the period, Charles Dickens was a major factor in giving the Victorian period its reputation for not only international power and wealth, but also humane social criticism and accomplished artistry.

To cast a larger historical perspective on the time period in which Charles Dickens lived and wrote, it may be helpful to think of him as a contemporary of Abraham Lincoln. Both reached the height of their mature accomplishment—Lincoln in politics, Dickens in literature—in the 1850s and 1860s, when they were in their forties and fifties. In 1860, Lincoln was elected president of the United States and Dickens began writing and publishing *Great Expectations.* Just as Lincoln's career was suddenly ended by assassination in 1865, Dickens finished his last complete novel, *Our Mutual Friend,* in that year (he started only one more novel, which he was unable to finish before his death five years later). Although neither man was completely happy in his private life, both Lincoln and Dickens became legendary figures while they were alive. Both have become representative democratic heroes of the nineteenth century: From humble beginnings they rose to greatness, and each gave new meaning to the struggle for human dignity.

FIVE CAREERS

Dickens was a man of extraordinary energy. His career as a novelist alone is remarkable in its own right. Most of his fifteen novels are close to a thousand pages long; *Great Expectations* is among the minority of shorter works. In addition to writing novels, however, he had a full-time career as a political journalist and champion of social reform, and as an editor, supervising a weekly publication for the last twenty years of his life. He continued to write accounts of his travels throughout his career as well, publishing four volumes of travel writing; and he had a lifelong involvement in the theater, regularly producing and acting in plays.

Along with his simultaneous careers as novelist, journalist, editor, and actor/theatrical producer, he frequently gave mesmerizing public readings of his work at home and abroad. None of this prevented him from having a highly developed domestic life as the head of a household of nine children, various in-laws, and numerous guests.

DICKENS'S BACKGROUND AND CHILDHOOD

Charles Dickens was born on February 7, 1812, in Portsmouth, England, about seventy miles southwest of London. His paternal grandparents had been illiterate servants. When his grandfather died and left behind several young children, and because his grandmother was fondly remembered by the family they served as a gifted storyteller, their son John—Dickens's father—was given a clerk's position in the navy pay office. This meant a rare chance to move up in society.

John Dickens extended his social progress by keeping his lowly family background a secret and courting and marrying Elizabeth Barrow, the daughter of a wealthy senior clerk in his office. But John's hopes of self-improvement took a blow when his father-in-law was accused of embezzlement, then confessed and fled, compounding his disgrace by abandoning his family. Thus the theme of rising precariously in society and being subject to sudden humiliating reversals—so central to *Great Expectations*—was prefigured by the experience of Charles Dickens's parents even before he was born.

His father was transferred to London when Dickens was two years old, then to Sheerness in Kent, and next to Chatham when he was five years old. Between the ages of five and ten, Dickens lived in Chatham with his family, and he remembered this five-year period for the rest of his life as a kind of paradise lost. Mrs. Dickens taught him to read, and

The house where Dickens was born in Portsmouth was humble, but a few months later the family had to move because they couldn't afford even this.

he started school at Giles Academy in 1821. Young Charles read passionately and widely before he was ten, especially popular English novels such as Daniel Defoe's *Robinson Crusoe* and Henry Fielding's *Tom Jones,* and others such as Miguel Cervantes's *Don Quixote.* Although he was somewhat sickly, Charles was outgoing and loved to perform with his beloved older sister Fanny and his four younger brothers and sisters when his parents entertained guests, as they frequently did. He even wrote a play at age nine, *Misnar, the Sultan of India,* for one of the family's home performances. It was a time of good cheer in the Dickens household. But this paradise was suddenly and forever lost when the family, in reduced circumstances, moved back to London in 1822.

One of the happy memories from this period Charles always cherished was of a walk he took with his father one day to nearby Gad's Hill (made famous by Shakespeare as Falstaff's locale in *Henry IV*). John Dickens pointed out a beautiful mansion, telling Charles that if he worked hard he could one day be rich and comfortable enough to live in such a home. Charles never forgot that. His own "great expectations" were thus put into concrete form, and the dream of rising from humble beginnings was passed on to the next generation.

Also during his five years in Chatham, the boy experienced nightmares, perhaps because of a nursemaid named Mary

Cherished memories of childhood were centered on the house in Chatham, where Dickens lived from 5 to 10 years old.

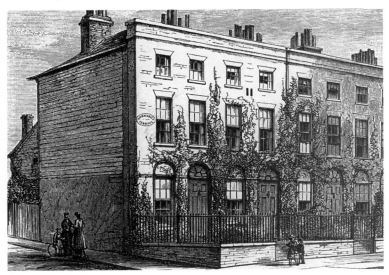

Weller, who told terrifying stories of a Captain Murderer who baked his wives in pies and ate them, or perhaps because of the frightening convict-workers in Chatham and the ominous hulks, or prison ship, on the river, where the convicts were taken at night. It is possible that the nightmares expressed fears and anxieties generated by his family's unstable lifestyle.

ON THE MOVE

John and Elizabeth Dickens, in their eagerness for comfort and social status, lived beyond their means. In addition to the household moves necessitated by their father's job as a navy clerk, the family was frequently uprooted to less expensive accommodations in an attempt to stay ahead of creditors. When John was transferred to London from Chatham, the ten-year-old Charles had already moved seven times. When the rest of the family left Chatham, Charles was left behind to finish three more months of school alone, compounding his insecurity and validating his fear of abandonment.

THE 1820S: THE SHOE POLISH FACTORY AND DEBTORS' PRISON

When he finally joined the family in London, Charles found his life suddenly changed. Living with six children and two parents in a four-room house in Camden Town, the Dickens family could no longer afford to send Charles to school. His sister's departure from home for music school left him again feeling abandoned, jealous, and resentful. Bill collectors hounded the family relentlessly. Mrs. Dickens tried to start a school but attracted not one student.

The family considered itself lucky when Charles, the oldest boy in the family, was offered a chance to go to work in a dilapidated shoe polish factory, Warren's Blacking. For twelve-year-old Charles this was a new low in his already painful existence. He later said:

> It is wonderful to me how I could have been so easily cast away at such an age. It is wonderful to me that, even after my descent into the poor little drudge I had been since we came to London, no one had compassion enough on me—a child of singular abilities: quick, eager, delicate, and soon hurt, bodily or mentally—to suggest that something might have been spared, as certainly it might have been, to place me at any common school.

For twelve hours a day, the boy put labels on pots of shoe polish inside the rat-infested warehouse. The work embedded grimy filth in his hands and under his fingernails that he found almost impossible to get off. Further, the physically small Charles was ostracized and degraded by contemptuous and crude coworkers. Based on this experience, the exploitation of children later became a major theme of Dickens's novels.

Only a week or two after he had begun this bitter work experience, Charles discovered things could get worse. His father was arrested for debt and thrown in jail. The family sold its possessions and moved into Marshalsea debtors' prison with the father—all except Charles, who roomed with a family friend while continuing to work at Warren's Blacking. Visiting his father in prison left a permanent impression, which he would re-create in novel after novel, of terrible suffering and the special horror of confinement of all kinds.

John Dickens was finally released from prison three months later, having inherited some money upon his mother's death. But he soon had Charles deliver an insulting letter he had written to the employer at Warren's Blacking, and as a result the boy was rudely fired from his wretched job. Charles's mother was angered by the loss of his meager income. He was returned to school for two and a half years at Wellington House Academy; however, not only was it a substandard school, but the satisfaction of resuming his studies was compromised by his mother's opposition to the idea and his feeling of being thus betrayed by her. "I never afterwards forgot," he said, "I never shall forget, I never can forget, that my mother was warm for my being sent back [to Warren's Blacking]."

When he was again removed from school at the age of fifteen because of new family debt, he went to work as an assistant at the law firm of Ellis and Blackmore. He was bored by legal technicalities and offended by the indifference of lawyers who profited from the misfortunes of others.

Determined again to rise in society despite his humiliations in the shoe polish factory and the debtors' prison, Dickens taught himself shorthand so he could become a court reporter, giving accounts of legal proceedings and trials. Later, as a self-taught political reporter, he recorded speeches given in Parliament, all while he was still a teenager. Soon he was able to quit the law office and find work as a freelance reporter. Dickens first sharpened his eye for detail and his powers of observation as a journalist, as many writers of realistic fiction have done. Upon turning eighteen, as soon as he was eligible, he acquired a reading ticket to the British Museum and resumed his education on his own.

THE 1830s: UPWARD STRUGGLE AND SUDDEN SUCCESS

Dickens wasted no time in trying to further his social progress by marrying a rich man's daughter as his father had. And also as his father had done, Charles kept his own low background a secret. He fell in love with a banker's daughter named Maria Beadnell, courting and pursuing her ardently for four years. He was ultimately rejected by Maria, after she had toyed with him throughout this period.

Shortly before he finally broke up with Maria Beadnell for good, he submitted a semifictional sketch of London life called "A Dinner at Poplar Walk" to the *Monthly Magazine,* and it was published. Dickens was neither paid nor given credit for the sketch, but he was thrilled to see his creative words in print. The magazine asked for more sketches and Dickens complied, adopting the pen name "Boz" as the author of these sketches. Boz was the Dickens family's nickname for his younger brother, who mispronounced his own name, Moses. In addition to writing newspaper accounts of speeches given in Parliament, Dickens continued to publish sketches using the name Boz for the next two years, and he was paid for his sketches by the *Evening Chronicle,* whose editor, George Hogarth, invited Dickens to his home and introduced him to his daughters.

Charles's determination to rise in society through marriage, though thwarted in the case of Maria Beadnell, was still intact—he soon became engaged to Hogarth's oldest daughter, Catherine, known by the nickname Kate. In 1836 the sketches were gathered together and published as a book, *Sketches by Boz.* Good reviews and sales followed, and Dickens was invited to write a long humorous book in twenty installments of the *Monthly Magazine,* which had published his first sketch. Thus his first novel, *Pickwick Papers,* began. Dickens celebrated his success by marrying Kate, two days after the first monthly installment of *Pickwick Papers* was published and two months after *Sketches by Boz.*

Although the first few monthly installments of the novel were not as popular as the sketches had been, Dickens's introduction of the character Sam Weller in the fourth installment made *Pickwick Papers* a sensation, read eagerly by people at all levels of English society. Dickens became a sudden dramatic success. (He still used the pen name Boz, although most readers knew his identity as the author.) He began a new serialized novel, *Oliver Twist,* while *Pickwick Papers* was still in progress. Whereas *Pickwick Papers* was humorous, *Oliver Twist* was a dark work of social criticism, focusing on the horrific aspects of institutional and urban street life, as experienced by an innocent and victimized orphan. Choosing an orphan as his main character was a pattern Dickens would return to in *Great Expectations.* With *Oliver Twist* Dickens appealed to readers' emotional sensibilities—the same audience that had been vastly amused by *Pickwick Papers* was aghast at the plight of the poor in society in *Oliver Twist.* His second novel was as popular as his first.

As soon as he finished *Pickwick Papers,* while *Oliver Twist* was only about half finished, Dickens began a third novel. *Nicholas Nickleby* combined the light comedy of *Pickwick* with the harsh social criticism of *Oliver,* this time focusing on the corruption of private boarding schools. Dickens's fourth novel, *The Old Curiosity Shop,* soon followed and established a new reputation for him as a writer of deep emotion and sentiment as well as humor and social criticism. When the heroine, Little Nell, became ill in the story, readers swamped the publisher's office with desperate but vain pleas not to let her die. Dickens followed *The Old Curiosity Shop* with *Barnaby Rudge,* a historical novel that was a departure for Dickens. Set in England at the time of the French Revolution, it represents an era Dickens would return to in *A Tale of Two Cities* eighteen years later. It was less popular than the first four novels, but overall, this initial phase of Dickens's career was characterized by extraordinary success.

Still in his twenties, he had written five successful novels in as many years, as well as a two-volume book of sketches and many newspaper accounts of politics and legal matters. In addition, he was an editor of magazines—*Bentley's Miscellany* in 1837 and *Master Humphrey's Clock* in 1840. Equally prolific at home, Dickens fathered four children during these years. Now rich and famous, he was invited to the most sophisticated occasions and events of high society, where he was warmly received. Because of the social criticism of his novels, Dickens was honored with an invitation from Baroness Angela Burdett-Coutts to advise her on philanthropic activity. He influenced her to fund such projects as the Home at Urania Cottage, Shepherd's Bush, a refuge for reformed prostitutes, as well as the demolition of slum housing in Bethnall Green and the building of the new Columbia Square model apartments in its place.

UNDER THE SURFACE

Dickens was exhausted from so much work, and he suffered from personal setbacks as well. When he married Kate, her younger sister Mary had come to live with them, and Dickens formed a close bond with her. When Mary suddenly died in 1838, Dickens, feeling abandoned yet again, was plunged into grief so intense that Kate became jealous. Mary's death was the inspiration for the heartrending death of Little Nell in *The Old Curiosity Shop*.

Kate was not outgoing or socially poised, and when Dickens was attending prestigious social events, she simply stayed home, intensifying his creeping dissatisfaction with marriage. Recognizing this, he took a year off from writing following this initial period of success, and he and Kate visited America as tourists in 1842, although she really did not enjoy traveling and would have preferred not to.

THE 1840s: RESTLESS YEARS

They visited Boston, Philadelphia, St. Louis, New York, and Washington, D.C. Everywhere they went, Dickens was surrounded by admiring crowds so overwhelming and unremitting that he felt smothered by his own fame, a downside of success. In addition he was disappointed to find many Americans boring and vain, in his opinion, and he was morally offended by slavery, which had been abolished in England ten years earlier. When he publicly complained of the lack of an international copyright law, which meant that others could publish his books without paying him, Dickens was accused of greed in the American press. After six months in America, Dickens returned to England and published his nonfiction *American Notes*, in which he tried to be polite and mask his unhappy experience in the United States. American critics were offended nevertheless.

In 1843 he published the immensely popular "A Christmas Carol" as one in a series of five annual Christmas stories. Then came the first installments of his sixth novel, *Martin Chuzzlewit*, in which he attacked America and its culture more directly, and even British readers reacted negatively to his bitterness. Following *Martin Chuzzlewit*, he traveled happily in Europe, recording the experience in *Pictures from Italy*, a nonfiction companion piece to his *American Notes*.

There was a restlessness in Dickens during these years. In addition to the two novels, the five Christmas stories, and the two travel books, he created and edited a liberal newspaper, the *Daily News*, and was deeply involved in the political issues of the day. But after seventeen issues of the paper, he passed it off to others. Also during this time, he produced and acted in amateur theatrical productions.

On the homefront, while Dickens's family was growing, his marriage was slowly but progressively deteriorating. Four more offspring joined the first four during the 1840s, but Dickens and Kate grew further apart. His restlessness expressed itself in flirtations with women he met socially, such as a Mrs. Colden, whom he met in New York in 1842. He even became temporarily infatuated with another woman named Christiana Weller in 1844, shortly before she married his close friend T.J. Thompson. But Kate became obsessively jealous in Italy in 1845, convinced that Charles was having an affair with a Mme. de la Rue. Dickens's inner turmoil caused insomnia during this period, and as a result his concentration and work habits suffered. His seventh novel, *Dombey and Son*, although successful, was written with uncharacteristic difficulty.

Added to this were painful personal experiences. First Dickens's beloved older sister Fanny died in 1848. Then Kate, after giving birth to Dora Annie, their ninth child, in 1850, had a nervous breakdown, and the child died less than a year later of what was called congestion of the brain. Kate was never able to resume charge of the household after this traumatic episode, and in that role she was replaced by her twenty-two-year-old sister, Georgina, who had been a member of the household for the preceding eight years. Also in 1851, shortly before the infant's death, Dickens's father, John, died.

During this period of losses, however, Dickens achieved an artistic turning point in his career with his eighth novel, *David Copperfield*, published in 1849–1850. For the first time, he conceived a hero who could survive in the midst of the problem-filled world of experience by using his artistic imagination, like Dickens himself. This autobiographical novel was a celebration of the artist's ability to cope with the world right in the center of it, as opposed to just surviving the world by retreating to some safe place at the edge of it, as Dickens's earlier heroes had done. In this way *David Copperfield* was optimistic and affirmative as well as very successful. It is ironic, then, that this novel ushered in Dickens's work of the 1850s, in which his vision of society and his criticism of it became both darker and more comprehensive.

THE 1850s: ARTISTIC ACCOMPLISHMENT AND PERSONAL SCANDAL

Bleak House (1852–1853), *Hard Times* (1854), and *Little Dorrit* (1856–1857), his ninth, tenth, and eleventh novels, broadened Dickens's attack on society, from specific social ills like orphanages in *Oliver Twist* and private boarding schools in

Nicholas Nickleby to institutions like the law itself in *Bleak House*, government in *Hard Times*, and the social class structure in *Little Dorrit*. At the same time, Dickens began to develop a more complex sense of the individual, who, in his view, is not only threatened by society but influenced by it. In his novels the individual must look within for society's influence and begin his reform there before he can change society itself. This new view of the individual would be fully realized at the end of the decade in *Great Expectations*.

Remarkably, Dickens founded and edited his own weekly, *Household Words*, in 1850, and he produced and acted in plays in 1851 and 1857. On top of his novels, journalism, and theatrical work, he added a new dimension. In 1853 he gave a public reading of "A Christmas Carol" as a benefit for charity, and thereafter he went on tour giving readings from his books in Europe, the United States, and throughout the British Isles.

Dickens's success reached a milestone in 1856 when he purchased Gad's Hill Place, the mansion his father had established in his mind as a symbol of material and social accomplishment when he was ten years old. The association of Shakespeare with Gad's Hill was indeed appropriate for Dickens, who, now in his forties, already was the second most famous and celebrated English writer of all time. "Successful" seems a hardly adequate description. The Dickens family moved into Gad's Hill Place in 1857.

But the tension between his successful external life and his troubled marriage finally gave way to open disarray. In 1858 Dickens and his wife formally separated after twenty-two years of marriage. Kate moved out of the Dickens household with twenty-one-year-old Charley, their oldest child, and the younger children remained with their father at Gad's Hill Place. Scandalous rumors ensued. According to one, Dickens was romantically linked with a teenage actress (hardly a respectable profession at that time, especially for women). To add to his anguish, Dickens suspected his mother-in-law was the source of this rumor. According to another, Dickens was involved with his own sister-in-law, Georgina Hogarth, who remained in his household after his wife had left.

The first rumor was factual, however. Dickens had met eighteen-year-old Ellen Ternan when they performed together in a play, and he fell passionately in love with her. Evidence has only recently come to light suggesting that Dickens maintained a romantic relationship with "Nelly" Ternan

Dickens wrote Great Expectations *in his study at Gad's Hill Place, the comfortable home that had represented social success to him since childhood.*

until his death thirteen years later. He provided her with a house in London, and she was a respected guest at Gad's Hill Place as well as a traveling companion when Dickens went to Paris in 1865. The true nature of their relationship remains unknown because the affair was conducted so discreetly. Dickens always insisted on the propriety of his relationship with Nelly, but he conducted it largely in secret, so much so that a great deal of detective work was required of author Claire Tomalin to piece together a biography of Nelly Ternan, published in 1991 and aptly titled *The Invisible Woman.*

Three years later, in writing of Pip's love for Estella in *Great Expectations*, Dickens was influenced by his experience with Nelly Ternan, according to scholars such as renowned Dickens biographer Edgar Johnson:

> It is inevitable that we should associate Pip's helpless enslavement to Estella with Dickens's desperate passion for Ellen Lawless Ternan. The very name "Estella" seems a kind of lawless anagram upon some of the syllables and initials of Ellen's name. . . . Never before had he portrayed a man's love for a woman with such emotional depth or revealed its desperation of compulsive suffering. . . . The unhappiness that breathes in Dickens's youthful letters to Maria Beadnell is the suffering of a boy, whereas Pip's is the stark misery of a man.

In 1859, less than a year after the initial scandal of the separation, Dickens started *All the Year Round*, a new weekly magazine, with the first installment of *A Tale of Two Cities*, his twelfth novel. The colorful setting of the French Revolution, the action and melodrama, and the theme of noble sacrifice made it one of his most popular novels ever. It has remained so, despite being viewed by critics as inferior to the three novels of the 1850s—*Bleak House, Hard Times,* and *Little Dorrit*—that preceded it.

A NEW AUTOBIOGRAPHICAL NOVEL

In 1860, as he began writing his thirteenth novel, *Great Expectations,* Dickens at forty-eight years old reviewed his life, beginning with his childhood. He had written the autobiographical *David Copperfield* ten years earlier, and those ten intervening years had darkened his view of the world and of himself, especially in the deepening realization that his own extraordinary success had not brought him personal happiness. He reread the earlier autobiographical novel to avoid repeating himself, but now, rather than the self-pity for his humble beginnings and the pride in his success with which he viewed himself in *David Copperfield,* he engaged in a new process of mature self-criticism and humility as he wrote.

This very self-criticism and humility in turn became a major theme of *Great Expectations;* in it he focused on the idea of personal development as a process of interaction with the world, not just passively learning about it by being virtuous and unchanging, as in *David Copperfield.* Although *Great Expectations* is less autobiographical than *David Copperfield,* it is a much more intense and probing revelation of his inner life. Dickens critic Monroe Engel sums up Dickens's progress between the two novels:

> *Great Expectations* provides a correction to the conventional optimism of *David Copperfield.* Pip must learn that fortune is not the way to happiness. Perhaps, too, Dickens is celebrating the losses that accompanied his success and the consequences of his will to forget his past. Certainly, to the modern reader, *Great Expectations* seems the more adult book—in its view of love, of success, of society.

While *Great Expectations* is a work of fiction, its narrator and main character, Pip, has a lot in common with Dickens. Like Pip, Dickens had a deprived and painful childhood that he was ashamed of. Like Pip, he had great expectations of escaping by moving up in society to a life of success and wealth, and also like Pip, he achieved it. But Dickens suffered terribly in love, and this, too, is Pip's experience. Most importantly, Dickens became disillusioned with his success in

society and his wealth. Finally he recognized the shallow-
ness of his own great expectations, and Pip learns and grows
in the novel in this same way.

WRITING *GREAT EXPECTATIONS*

When Dickens first began work on *Great Expectations*, he intended to write it in twenty monthly installments. But the
weekly he was editing, *All the Year Round*, was doing badly fi-
nancially, so he decided to issue it in shorter weekly installments with a shorter, more compact overall length. Because
of this constraint, the novel is more artistically constructed

The character Miss Havisham in Great Expectations *is a good example of Dickens's tendency toward the grotesque. A jilted bride, she
is both pathetic and monstrous.*

and concentrated in its effect than most of his longer and more loosely organized novels. According to J. Hillis Miller, one of the most respected modern Dickens critics, "What it took Dickens in 1850 the first hundred pages of *David Copperfield* to say is presented far more powerfully in the first few pages of *Great Expectations.*"

In *Great Expectations* Dickens attempted to return to the light humor that had distinguished his early novels like *Pickwick Papers* and that had been notably absent from his later *A Tale of Two Cities.* In a letter to a friend, Dickens said, "You will not have to complain of the want of humour, as in the *Tale of Two Cities.* I have made the opening, I hope, in its general effect exceedingly droll. I have put a child and a good-natured foolish man, in relations that seem to me very funny." But Dickens's memories of his childhood also included nightmares, and from the beginning, the inspiration for *Great Expectations* was a "grotesque tragi-comic conception." Although there is significant humor throughout *Great Expectations,* ultimately it is only a part of a more serious and complex vision.

THE CONTROVERSIAL ENDING

As Dickens originally wrote the ending of the novel, Estella and Pip meet by chance years after the story ends. Pip feels that she has come to understand through her own experience some of the pain she has caused him, but the impression is that they will not meet again. Dickens's friend and fellow novelist Bulwer Lytton objected that this ending was too harsh, and Dickens allowed himself to be convinced to change it so that Pip and Estella could end up together.

Many critics, including the great British playwright George Bernard Shaw, have felt that the original ending was more honest and less sentimental. "Dickens put nearly all his thought into [*Great Expectations*]," Shaw said. "It is too serious a book to be a trivially happy one. Its beginning is unhappy; its middle is unhappy; and the conventional happy ending is an outrage on it." Critics who focus on the false social values represented by Estella believe that in order for Pip to see through these false values, he must ultimately be free of her. As Edgar Johnson puts it, "Both as art and as psychology it was poor counsel that Lytton gave in urging that the shaping of a lifetime in Estella be miraculously undone."

On the other hand, many critics, particularly those whose focus is Pip's moral growth, prefer the revised ending. J. Hillis Miller writes:

Pip and Estella have experienced before their union their most complete separation, Pip in the agony of discovery that Estella is not destined for him and that Magwitch is his real benefactor, and Estella in her unhappy marriage to Bentley Drummle, who has "used her with great cruelty," just as Pip has been "used" by Estella. These experiences have transformed them both. . . . Both have come back from a kind of death to meet and join in the moonlight in Miss Havisham's ruined garden. The second ending is, in my opinion, the best. Not only was it, after all, the one Dickens published . . . but, it seems to me, the second ending, in joining Pip and Estella, is much truer to the real direction of the story.

Such controversy invites each reader to decide for himself or herself which ending seems most appropriate to the novel as a whole. The wide diversity of opinion demonstrated in this collection on the ending and other issues in *Great Expectations* is meant to stimulate each reader to appreciate this powerful novel as fully as possible and according to one's own experience and understanding.

THE FINAL YEARS

Three years after completing *Great Expectations*, Dickens began the monthly installments of his fourteenth and last complete novel, *Our Mutual Friend* (1864–1865). Like his highly regarded novels of the 1850s, it is remarkably complete and rich—but it is even darker in its portrait of a corrupt society. In it, a modern industrial wasteland is represented by London's garbage dumps and polluted river.

Throughout the 1860s, Dickens exhausted himself giving public readings of his beloved works in London, Paris, Scotland, and Ireland. One notable tour stands out: In 1867 he made a triumphal return to America, where his readings were well received. Despite his warm reception, his opinions of America remained basically unchanged, however, although he was more polite about it after twenty-five years. He continued his public touring in England upon his return and began a fifteenth novel, *The Mystery of Edwin Drood*, in 1869.

Edwin Drood was never finished and the mystery never solved because Dickens died of a stroke on June 9, 1870, at the age of fifty-eight. At the time of his death, he was living in the mansion at Gad's Hill. Charles Dickens was buried as a national hero in the Poet's Corner of Westminster Abbey, where his tombstone identifies him as "England's most popular author."

CHAPTER 1

Major Themes in *Great Expectations*

READINGS ON
GREAT EXPECTATIONS

Enjoy Dickens with Me

Eldred J. Wilden

Eldred J. Wilden was an eighteen-year-old student in New Zealand when he wrote this essay after reading *Great Expectations*. In it he surveys some of the themes of the novel that would strike a first-time reader. He remarks on the novel's discussion of happiness and social ambition, the atmosphere of secrecy and mystery, the recurring imagery of light and darkness, the cast of vivid characters, and the novel's humorous incidents and complex ending.

Ever since the novel was first written in the early eighteenth century, the reading public has delighted in this literary form. The essential features of the novel, the author's vision of life, the pervading atmosphere, the distinctive characterisation, the style of writing are what give lasting enjoyment to readers. A book which I consider has all these elements of pleasurable reading is *Great Expectations* by that great storyteller, Charles Dickens. I am now going to elaborate on the characteristics of this book and I ask you to "enjoy Dickens with me."

The theme of *Great Expectations* draws attention to what constitutes true happiness and true gentlemanliness in the story of a poor boy, Pip, and his expectations of wealth and happiness. This theme is of universal interest because nearly everyone seeks happiness and wealth. The reader follows the career of Pip as he endeavours to become a gentleman, using the money given to him by an unknown benefactor. Pip is naturally decent, but ambition leads him into selfishness, moral cowardice, and all the outward trappings of snobbery. He ignores his best friend, Joe, and is embarrassed by him in the presence of his upper-class associates, Miss Havisham and Herbert Pocket. Yet when Pip is ill and in need of a friend, it is Joe who forgives and forgets and nurses him back to health. In these incidents, Dickens

Reprinted from "Enjoy Dickens with Me," by Eldred J. Wilden, *The Dickensian*, vol. 62, no. 350, Autumn 1966, pp. 185–87.

makes the reader, as well as Pip, face the truth—that happiness is not gained by wealth and that the true gentleman is not the snobbish Pip but the humble Joe.

A NOVEL OF MYSTERIES

Mystery and secrecy pervade this novel. Pip himself is a repository of secrets from the opening chapter, when he becomes the unwilling accomplice of a runaway convict, to the time when he tracks down Estella's parentage. His own career is a secret and in secret he starts Herbert on his career. In Jagger's office, infinite precautions are taken to prevent secrets from leaking out and the habit of secrecy is comically maintained by Wemmick at his marriage, the wedding ceremony being disguised as a fishing expedition. The greatest mystery of all is the identity of Pip's benefactor. It comes as an unexpected surprise to learn that the benefactor is not Miss Havisham, but Magwitch.

The contrasting atmosphere throughout the book adds to its appeal. There is considerable play of light and shadow. The bright prospects of Pip are overshadowed by the dark scheming of Miss Havisham, Orlick and Compeyson. The half-light of the mists on the marshes, the artificial light of the gas-lamps in the London streets and the candles at Satis House help to emphasise the falseness and dishonesty of many of the characters. The bright sunshine in which Pip talks to Biddy and Herbert emphasises their honesty and frankness. The use of sound is effective, particularly the slight noises heard in an oppressive stillness. The rasping of the file in the eerie stillness of the marshes, the mice behind the panels of Satis House, the nocturnal creakings in the Hummums, the mysterious ripples as the fugitives creep down the river in the dark, stir the imagination and give dramatic tenseness.

Characters impart life and vitality to a novel and in *Great Expectations*, Dickens portrays a set of unforgettable characters opening up new fields of enjoyment to his readers. Magwitch, the hunted fugitive, whose aim is to make Pip a gentleman, is one of Dickens's greatest creations from humble life. Miss Havisham, the bride deserted on her wedding day, fascinates readers. She still wears her wedding frock and is surrounded by the remains of the intended wedding feast. She uses Pip as the instrument of her revenge against men and leads him, quite innocently, to believe that she is his unknown benefactor. The hidden villain, Compeyson, the formidable lawyer, Jaggers, and his efficient clerk, Wemmick, are a contrast to the self-effacing Joe and the shrewd placid Biddy. One of the most intriguing characters of the book is the beautiful Estella, the adopted daughter of Miss Havisham. She is trained from early childhood to break men's hearts. Pip is her victim when he first meets her and is made to realise that he is coarse and common. He is her victim, too, in adult life, but the reader feels that there is something pathetic in Estella's heartlessness and consequent loneliness. Pip, the hero, is introduced as a "small bundle of shivers." He is baited and bullied by his elders, with the exception of Joe, and throughout his boyhood suffers a perpetual conflict with injustice. In young manhood, he lives in a world of make-believe and self-deception until he finds his true identity in love and unselfish loyalty.

A host of minor characters help to bring this book to life and provide some of the humour which lightens the serious and symbolic content of the story. Examples of this lighter vein are Trabb's boy mimicking Pip as he sees him in his fine new clothes and Mr. Wopsle's performance as Hamlet.

Dickens wrote with huge enjoyment. His literary training was imperfect but his faults and mannerisms are swallowed up in the zest with which he arrests the attention of his readers. Dickens had started his public readings in 1858 and parts of *Great Expectations* seem to have been written with an eye on future declamation. The book is sprinkled with passages that would recite well and with character sketches that lend themselves to humorous impersonation. The scene in which Magwitch stands trial shows Dickens at his best. It is colourful and in its detailed realism gives a vivid contrast between human depravity and human dignity.

A SATISFYING ENDING

I feel readers are pleased that this book ends happily. Dickens at first had planned otherwise. He had made Estella a cold young woman and Pip a very warm-hearted young man. Pip had been disappointed in his expectations and had not even secured the hand of Biddy, but Dickens evidently felt that these set-backs were no less than he deserved. He had intended, too, that Pip and Estella should remain apart, but on the advice of a fellow novelist, he changed the ending. Miss Havisham, Estella's evil genius, was dead; the past was dead and it was not too much to expect that the old hard Estella was dead too. The last words of the book leave readers with the quiet suggestion that all will end happily for Pip and that he will marry Estella. "I saw no shadow of another parting from her," says Pip, although Estella had just said that they would "continue friends apart."

If you have read *Great Expectations* I hope you have enjoyed remembering it with me. If you have not yet read it, I hope you feel it is a "must" on your reading list. *Great Expectations* is one of Charles Dickens's finest novels for it has the excitement, the mystery, the humour enjoyed alike by young and old.

The Theme of Love and Money

Keith Selby

Great Expectations is commonly described with the German word Bildungsroman. A Bildungsroman is a novel that focuses on the education or development of the central character, in this case Pip. Writer and poet Keith Selby emphasizes the way Pip changes and grows in the course of the novel, by learning about the world and by interacting with Dickens's various characters. In reviewing the plot, Selby finds human relationships corrupted by money, which makes Pip's learning process complex and painful. The novel's opening scene illustrates that connection with others is crucial to creating a personal identity, and the fates of Miss Havisham, Mrs. Joe, and Orlick indicate the result of corrupted relationships.

Great Expectations belongs to the type of novel known as a *Bildungsroman*, or education novel. The phrase I shall use to describe it is 'education novel', but I mention the German term *Bildungsroman* (which means the same thing) because you may well encounter it if you read other critical works about *Great Expectations*. Broadly speaking, the education novel tells the story of the personal and moral development of its central character. By the end of the novel this central character has learnt something about the world or about himself or herself, and has become a very different person from the one we first met in the novel's opening.

CONSTRUCTING AN OVERALL ANALYSIS

In *Great Expectations* the central character is Pip, and he tells his story from the point of view of his adulthood, looking back over the events which have formed his character. All this has certain implications for the form of the novel: be-

Excerpted from *How to Study a Charles Dickens Novel*, by Keith Selby. Copyright © 1989 by Keith Selby. Reprinted with permission from Macmillan Press Ltd.

cause Pip tells his own story directly to the reader, we have the impression of being able to see into his mind as he speaks. . . . But the first thing to do is to organise your response to the text itself, as this will enable you to build your own view of the novel. The place to start, as always, is with some thoughts about the novel's plot.

After reading the novel, think about the story and what kind of pattern you can see in the plot. Great Expectations tells the story of Philip Pirrip, known as 'Pip', an orphan brought up by his bad-tempered sister and her warmhearted husband, Joe Gargery, the village blacksmith.

As a child, Pip is confronted by an escaped convict on the marshes, and the convict—Abel Magwitch—forces Pip to bring him food and a file. Magwitch is recaptured, however, after a struggle with another escaped convict, Compeyson, and both are returned to their prison ship. Some time later Pip is sent for by Miss Havisham, who, having been jilted on her wedding-day many years previously, has lived cut off from society in her home, Satis House, ever since. Miss Havisham has an adopted daughter, the beautiful Estella, whom she has brought up as a cold, heartless child to wreak her revenge on men. Pip falls in love with Estella but she immediately rebuffs him, and as a result he begins to despise his lowly origins. When Pip is fourteen, Miss Havisham pays for him to be apprenticed to Joe Gargery, the village blacksmith, and his visits to Satis House and to Estella come to an end.

Four years into his apprenticeship Pip receives a visit from an Old Bailey lawyer, Jaggers, whom he had met at Satis House some years previously. Jaggers has been sent to tell him that he has ready money to make Pip a gentleman, and expectations of great wealth for him. The money comes from an unknown benefactor, and the only condition attached to it is that Pip must never attempt to discover the identity of this unknown benefactor. Pip immediately assumes his benefactor to be Miss Havisham, and assumes also that she is preparing him to be a gentleman so that he may in time marry Estella. He goes to London to learn to be a gentleman. There he becomes friends with Herbert Pocket, a nephew of Miss Havisham's, whom he had previously met at Satis House.

In London, Pip becomes proud and snobbish and neglects his old friends, but particularly the loving blacksmith, Joe Gargery. He gradually gets himself further and further into debt, and is continually snubbed by Estella, who is now also living in London. It is at this point that Pip's real benefactor is revealed. This turns out to be Abel Magwitch, the convict he helped on the marshes when he was a child, and who has in the meantime made a fortune as a transported convict in Australia. Pip at first rejects the lowly Magwitch, and is ashamed that the source of his present wealth comes from a criminal. Pip learns that Estella has married the boorish Bentley Drummle, and this throws him further into the depths of depression.

Magwitch is finally recaptured when he is betrayed by his old enemy Compeyson, and is sentenced to death. But he dies before he can be executed. Pip is left penniless, although he has discovered that Magwitch is Estella's father, that her real mother is Jaggers's housekeeper, and that Compeyson is the lover who jilted Miss Havisham on her wedding-day. After a long illness in which he is nursed patiently by Joe, who also pays off his debts, Pip sees the idle foolishness of his previous way of life and returns to his home village, intent on asking Biddy, a childhood friend, to marry him.

But on his return to the blacksmith's home he discovers Biddy and Joe on their wedding-day, and determines to put his own life in order by going to work as a clerk for the company in which Herbert is now a partner. Eleven years later he visits the ruins of Satis House (Miss Havisham is now dead), where he meets Estella. Mistreated by Drummle, Estella is now a widow and a reformed, affectionate woman. Their hands clasp, with the promise of love, happiness and marriage in the inevitable future—at least in one version of the novel's ending. . . .

RELATIONSHIPS CORRUPTED BY MONEY

The way to start making sense of a novel is to look for some type of pattern in the plot. This pattern can take many forms, but a good rule of thumb is to look for a situation, or a particular type of character, or a particular relationship between characters being repeated several times. Remember, though, that in a Dickens novel the overall pattern we can expect to find will eventually focus upon a conflict or tension between money and love. This applies even where, as here, we have a fairly long and intricate plot. This in itself, however, can tell us a great deal about the novel.

One of the reasons why the plot is so complicated is that it is being reported by the first-person narrator, Pip, and Pip —unlike an omniscient narrator—cannot know everything about all the characters and all their relationships. The result of this is that things are gradually discovered, both by the reader and by Pip. What gradually comes out in Pip's story is that many of the characters are either unwittingly related to each other (Magwitch, for instance, being Estella's father) or want to keep their relationships secret. When Pip is in London, for example, posing as a gentleman, he wants to keep his relationship with Joe Gargery a secret from his new friends, the Finches of the Grove. Similarly, Herbert Pocket has to keep his relationship with Clara a secret because he knows his snobbish mother will not approve of her. What we have to ask ourselves is how all these secret relationships illustrate something about the conflict between love and money.

We can begin by thinking about the concept of a relationship between people. Normally, this has to do with family ties, or sexual and emotional ties between people. One of its identifying characteristics is that it has to do with feelings, with love for another person. Why then, should so many of the relationships in *Great Expectations* have to be kept a secret? The simple answer is: money.

Think, for example, of the various secret benefactors in the novel. Pip believes that Miss Havisham is his secret benefactor, when in fact it is Magwitch—but Pip can ask no questions, since it must be kept a secret. Later Pip arranges, with Miss Havisham as a secret benefactor, to establish Herbert in business—but the whole thing must be kept a secret. One of the reasons for wanting to be a benefactor is presumably a desire to help somebody by giving them money. But in all the cases in the novel—with the notable exception of Joe, who openly pays off Pip's debts—to give financial help to somebody means hiding who you are, and hiding your relationship to that person. In other words, the thing which intervenes between characters in most of the relationships in the novel is money. Money actually obscures the expression of love, and this is a major theme in the novel. What is particularly interesting, however, is that all the characters have the need for love and for a relationship with another person, but this is consistently obscured by financial considerations.

In such a situation characters become utilities: Estella is handed over to Miss Havisham by Jaggers to save her mother from the gallows; Pip is bought off by Miss Havisham when she has finished toying with his emotions, and made Joe's apprentice; even Compeyson's jilting of Miss Havisham was motivated by money. Looked at in this way, the whole novel can be seen to stem from a basic conflict between love and money, and it is this conflict which occupies Pip in his narrative. When he goes to London he leaves Joe's natural love and simplicity of spirit behind him. But in London, and although he has ready money in his pocket, his snobbishness forces him to keep his relationship with Joe a secret; he is snubbed by Estella, disdained by the Finches, and ultimately without love because he is emotionally alone. What this suggests is that all people, no matter what material wealth they possess, need the love and friendship of other people, but that money can make that love and friendship impossible to have.

Analyse the opening paragraph or two of the novel and try to build on the ideas you have established so far. Once you have identified the conflict which is at the centre of *Great Expectations,* the next stage is to look at the opening of the novel itself, since it is here that Dickens's unique handling of the topic is going to be most apparent. This is how the novel starts:

> My father's family name being Pirrip, and my christian name Philip, my infant tongue could make of both names nothing longer or more explicit than Pip. So, I called myself Pip, and came to be called Pip.
>
> I give Pirrip as my father's family name, on the authority of his tombstone and my sister—Mrs Joe Gargery, who married the blacksmith. As I never saw my father or my mother, and never saw any likeness of either of them (for their days were long before the days of photographs), my fancies regarding what they were like, were unreasonably derived from their tombstones.

The first thing to do with this passage is, as always, to find some form of opposition or tension within it. The passage itself is straightforward enough: it introduces the novel's central character, Pip. But if you think about the way in which it does that, you will immediately notice that there is a tension of some kind between Pip the child and the family of which he should be a part. That is, this child can report who he is only on the basis of fragmentary evidence gleaned from inanimate or distant sources: 'I give Pirrip as my father's family name, on the authority of his tombstone.' He has no father to tell him anything, no mother, not even an image of them, 'for their days were long before the days of photographs'. Even his one surviving relative—his sister—is in a sense no relative to him at all, since even she does not share his name: 'and my sister—Mrs Joe Gargery'.

You might be tempted to argue that all the passage tells us is that Pip is an orphan. But this would be to miss all the details of the text, and to miss how the passage relates to the novel as a whole. If we now extend the idea that here we have a child curiously isolated from the family of which he should be a part, we should begin to see how the passage focuses on the novel's central themes.

For example, not only is this child wholly alone in the world, but he literally does not know who he is. Since he has no family he has no relation to anything at all. Consequently, he is forced into the situation of having to provide himself with a name: 'I called myself Pip, and came to be called Pip'. A child's name is normally provided by the parents, and that assumes a child's relationship with the past and a personal, family history to support it. But Pip has no past, and hence no relationship to anything. Consequently, not only does he possess nothing (and much of *Great Expectations* is about the desire to possess), but he also has no status in the world, because he is wholly alienated from it. He has no place anywhere, and is nobody. We could safely project from this that much of the novel will have to do with Pip trying to become somebody, trying to discover who he is. The only way in which he can do this, as the above passage suggests, is by building relationships with other people, since he has none to start with. The effect of the passage as a whole, then, is that it impresses very forcefully on our minds a sense of Pip's isolation in the world, and the need for him to build relationships with other people in order to discover who he is. The novel details his successes and failures in this quest to discover a person in himself and a position in the world. . . .

JOE AND PIP

Select a second passage for discussion. The only loving relationship in which we see Pip in the early part of the novel is with Joe Gargery, his sister's husband. Any passage in which he and Pip appear together will tell you a lot about the closeness of their simple relationship, but it may be more productive to look at Pip and Joe together being confronted by another character who is not a part of their relationship. The extract I have chosen describes Joe and Pip at Satis House, where they have been summoned by Miss Havisham, who plans to pay for Pip to be apprenticed to Joe:

> 'Have you brought his indentures with you?' asked Miss Havisham.
>
> 'Well, Pip, you know,' replied Joe, as if that were a little unreasonable, 'you yourself see me put 'em in my 'at, and therefore you know as they are here.' With which he took them

---

DICKENS'S INSPIRATION AND PLAN FOR
GREAT EXPECTATIONS

When he first conceived of Great Expectations, *Dickens was thinking of the unfolding process of learning by living—of a central character/narrator who would begin as a child and evolve first into an apprentice and then an adult. The title was in place, and Dickens saw the potential for humor in this story, but he also saw it as "grotesque" and tragic. These comments come from letters Dickens wrote to his close friend and biographer John Forster.*

For a little piece I have been writing—or am writing; for I hope to finish it to-day—such a very fine, new, and grotesque idea has opened upon me, that I begin to doubt whether I had not better cancel the little paper, and reserve the notion for a new book. You shall judge as soon as I get it printed. But it so opens out before *me* that I can see the whole of a serial revolving on it, in a most singular and comic manner. . . .

The book will be written in the first person throughout, and during these first three weekly numbers you will find the hero to be a boy-child, like David. Then he will be an apprentice. You will not have to complain of the want of humour as in the *Tale of Two Cities.* I have made the opening, I hope, in its general effect exceedingly droll. I have put a child and a good-natured foolish man, in relations that seem to me very funny. Of course I have got in the pivot on which the story will turn too—and which indeed, as you remember, was the grotesque tragi-comic conception that first encouraged me. To be quite sure I had fallen into no unconscious repetitions, I read *David Copperfield* again the other day, and was affected by it to a degree you would hardly believe.

John Forster, *The Life of Charles Dickens.* 2 vols. (London: J.M. Dent & Sons, 1966 reprint), II, pp. 284–85.

out, and gave them, not to Miss Havisham, but to me. I am afraid I was ashamed of the dear good fellow—I *know* I was ashamed of him—when I saw that Estella stood at the back of Miss Havisham's chair, and that her eyes laughed mischieviously. I took the indentures out of his hand and gave them to Miss Havisham.

'You expected,' said Miss Havisham, as she looked them over, 'no premium with the boy?'

'Joe!' I remonstrated; for he made no reply at all.

'Why don't you answer—'

'Pip,' returned Joe, cutting me short as if he were hurt, 'which I meantersay that were not a question requiring a answer betwixt yourself and me, and which you know the answer to be full well No. You know it to be No, Pip, and wherefore should I say it?'

Miss Havisham glanced at him as if she understood what he really was, better than I had thought possible, seeing what he was there; and took up a little bag from the table beside her.

'Pip has earned a premium here,' she said, 'and here it is. There are five-and-twenty guineas in this bag. Give it to your master, Pip.'

Before I start on the analysis of this passage, I want to remind you that I am mainly concerned in this book with illustrating a method of analysing a novel. An important part of this method has to do with noticing the novelist's use of particular techniques or patterns, so don't forget that techniques or patterns you notice in one novel will probably recur in other novels, and will function in much the same way. This can give you a starting-point for your analysis of other, apparently quite dissimilar passages from quite different novels. The use of one such technique can be seen in the above passage.

Do you remember how in *Hard Times* Dickens draws attention to the gulf between the world of love and the world of money by having his characters speak very differently? In that novel, the inhabitants of the world of love (represented by Sleary's circus) speak a language which deviates from normal expression. What we can notice in the above passage is that Joe, like Sleary, uses language in a way which is again deviant. This should awaken us to the fact that Joe is in some way outside ordered and conventional society. His view of the world, as the above passage demonstrates, is one based upon a simple love for his fellow men, and this is brought out in the way he speaks a language other than that used by the inhabitants of the world of money. Using this as a springboard into analysis of this passage, we can immediately see that there is a tension between the world of love (represented by Joe), and the world of money (represented by Miss Havisham and Estella). Between these two we find Pip, who is in some way related to both. And this directs our attention to a more specific tension: Pip's relation to Joe, on the one hand, and his relation to Miss Havisham and Estella, on the other.

To pull these ideas together, then, we can say that the tension in this passage is in the relationship between the various characters and Pip, the subject of the transaction. That it is a transaction is well worth keeping in mind, for it is this which provides the focus of the tensions within the passage. These tensions all bear down upon Pip, whom each character regards differently: to Joe, the relationship is simple—he loves Pip dearly; to Miss Havisham, Pip is a utility who has 'earned a premium', and now she has finished with him she is selling him off to another master—'Give it to your master, Pip', she says, meaning Joe; and to Estella, Pip, whom she now regards from behind Miss Havisham's chair, is an object of disdain, the 'common labouring boy' she treated 'as insolently as if he were a dog in disgrace'. Having identified this general tension between the characters in the passage as a whole, the thing to do now is to look at the details of the passage and to consider how these reinforce this tension.

To take Joe's relationship with Pip first. The most striking thing about Joe's response to the situation is that he replies not to Miss Havisham, but to Pip. This in itself is immediately amusing, and there are all sorts of ways in which we can account for it naturalistically. There is every reason to assume that this simple village blacksmith is understandably in awe of this strange woman in her strange house. But, as always, and although we can account for the situation naturalistically, Joe's response also fits in with the thematic tensions of the passage and of the novel as a whole. When Miss Havisham tries to confirm with Joe that he expected 'no premium for the boy', Joe fails to answer. The reason for this is plain: he doesn't answer because he has no answer. As he tells Pip, it 'were not a question requiring an answer betwixt yourself and me'. Joe is unnerved and affronted not only by Miss Havisham's strange appearance, but also by what he sees as her strange desire to turn his relationship with Pip into a commercial one. In refusing to talk directly to Miss Havisham, he is refusing to share in her view of the world, refusing to turn his love for Pip into a commercial transaction.

Miss Havisham and Estella, on the other hand, share in their view of Pip only as an object—a point reinforced by the fact that they both see him, quite literally, from the same position: 'Estella stood at the back of Miss Havisham's chair'. Their relationship to Pip and Joe, signalled by the physical distance between them, is the relationship of master to servant; Miss Havisham, for example, is insistent that—as she says a little later—'Gargery is your [Pip's] new master now', implying, therefore, that she was his master previously. Just as Joe cannot conceive of a relationship based upon economic principles, so Miss Havisham and Estella are unable to conceive of a relationship based upon love. This conflict has massive implications for Pip's relationship with Joe, and marks a turning-point in his career.

This can be seen most obviously in the way Pip describes Joe. Previously, he has told us that his love for Joe was a simple matter of equality: 'I had always treated Joe as a larger species of child, and as no more than my equal'. Now, however, that he is the subject of a commercial transaction, and confronted by the world of money represented by Miss Havisham, Pip's simple love for Joe is replaced by shame: 'I am afraid to say I was ashamed of the dear good fellow—I *know* I was ashamed of him.' But not only is Pip ashamed of Joe; he suddenly enters into a new relationship with him, the relationship of master and servant. On the one hand, Joe, as Miss Havisham insists, is Pip's new 'master'; but, on the other, and as Pip now sees Joe, he is a socially inept fool, and somebody to be ashamed of in front of Miss Havisham and Estella. This tension, then, between Pip and Joe, on the one hand, and Pip, Estella and Miss Havisham, on the other, underpins the more general tension in the novel as a whole between the world of love and the world of money, for it is the pernicious effect of money upon people and relationships which destroys the simple love Pip had previously held for Joe. . . .

EVEN THE LOWLY ORLICK CRAVES LOVE

One of the things that we can see already is that the novel explores the many facets of the relationships that exist between people. It does this by setting love in conflict with money, and demonstrates the pernicious effect of money upon people and upon their ability to care for another person. What makes the novel particularly interesting, however, is that in exploring the nature of love between people it is able to explore some of the darker areas of the human mind, because love itself operates irrationally. For example, there is a great deal in Miss Havisham with which we can sympathise, because we know the sadness of her past. But it is in her response to the past that we lose sympathy with her. In a sense, she attempts to rationalise a situation which is really beyond rationalisation. Consequently, she chooses to use love—in her case thwarted love—as a lever upon other people, and to use love in this way is ultimately destructive.

What is worth remembering is that much the same is going to be true even of minor characters in the novel, such as Orlick and Mrs Joe. Mrs Joe is forever reminding Pip how fortunate he is to have been brought up 'by hand', and how many sacrifices she has made on his behalf, reinforcing these sacrifices with the necessary application of 'Tickler', a wax-ended piece of cane. The following confrontation between Mrs Joe, Tickler and Pip demonstrates the point:

> 'Where have you been, you young monkey?' said Mrs Joe, stamping her foot. 'Tell me directly what you've been doing to wear me away with fret and fright and worrit, or I'd have you out of that corner if you was fifty Pips, and he was five hundred Gargerys.'
>
> 'I have only been to the churchyard,' said I, from my stool, crying and rubbing myself.
>
> 'Churchyard!' repeated my sister. 'If it warn't for me you'd have been to the churchyard long ago, and stayed there. Who brought you up by hand?'
>
> 'You did,' said I.
>
> 'And why did I do it, I should like to know?' exclaimed my sister.
>
> I whimpered, 'I don't know.'
>
> 'I don't!' said my sister. 'I'd never do it again! I know that. I may truly say I've never had this apron of mine off, since born you were. It's bad enough to be a blacksmith's wife (and him a Gargery) without being your mother.'
>
> My thoughts strayed from that question as I looked disconsolately at the fire. For, the fugitive out on the marshes with the ironed leg, the mysterious young man, the file, the food, and the dreadful pledge I was under to commit a larceny on those sheltering premises, rose before me in the avenging coals.

This scene occurs directly after Pip's meeting with Magwitch in the churchyard, a scene which demonstrates Pip's isolation in the world, and his desire for parental love. The contrast between Pip's need for parental love and a home, and this confrontation with Mrs Joe, his adoptive mother in her home, sums up much of what the novel is about: characters are alone in the world and need the love and affection of others, but this must be freely given, not bought by money or forced out by threats.

We can see here, however, that Mrs Joe expects Pip's gratitude and love, without expending any herself—just as Miss Havisham expects Estella's love, even after having killed Estella's capacity for love. What all this is based upon is love by reward, love with a price-tag on it. It works through the operation of guilt, and Pip senses this guilt keenly: 'the pledge I was under to commit a larceny on those sheltering premises, rose before me in the avenging coals'. Mrs Joe's method is emotional blackmail plain and simple, and, just as distorted passion eventually destroys Miss Havisham, so Mrs Joe is eventually killed by the same distorted passion. It is this which, much later, Orlick, 'shaking his head and hugging himself', tells us drove him to attempt to kill both Mrs Joe and Pip: 'You [Pip] was favoured, and he [Orlick] was bullied and beat'. Even the lowly Orlick craves love, and, in being deprived of it, his craving turns into violence and hatred.

Or, at least, that is the conclusion I draw. Your examination of the evidence might lead you to see things differently.

The Theme of Original Sin

Dorothy Van Ghent

Dorothy Van Ghent is the author of *The English Novel: Form and Function*, a highly regarded critical study of British fiction. Here, she examines the opening scene of *Great Expectations*. Pip's initial confrontation with Magwitch figuratively and literally turns his world upside down, and Dickens vividly conveys the confusion, the shock, and the loneliness of new awareness. Magwitch's sudden appearance in the first chapter and Pip's identification with him introduce the novel's major psychological theme—the sense of inherited guilt, or "original sin," which is basic to the human condition.

[*Great Expectations*] opens with a child's first conscious experience of his aloneness. Immediately an abrupt encounter occurs—Magwitch suddenly comes from behind a gravestone, seizes Pip by the heels, and suspends him upside down.

> "Hold your noise!" cried a terrible voice, as a man started up from among the graves at the side of the church porch. "Keep still, you little devil, or I'll cut your throat!"

Perhaps, if one could fix on two of the most personal aspects of Dickens' technique, one would speak of the strange languages he concocts for the solitariness of the soul, and the abruptness of his tempo. His human fragments suddenly shock against one another in collisions like those of Democritus' atoms or of the charged particles of modern physics. Soldiers, holding out handcuffs, burst into the blacksmith's house during Christmas dinner at the moment when Pip is clinging to a table leg in an agony of apprehension over his theft of the pork pie. A weird old woman clothed in decayed satin, jewels and spider webs, and with one shoe off, shoots out her finger at the bewildered child, with the command:

Excerpts adapted from *The English Novel: Form and Function*, by Dorothy Van Ghent. Copyright 1953 by Dorothy Van Ghent and renewed 1981 by Roger Van Ghent. Reprinted by permission of Holt, Rinehart and Winston.

"Play!" A pale young gentleman appears out of a wilderness of cucumber frames, and daintily kicking up his legs and slapping his hands together, dips his head and butts Pip in the stomach. These sudden confrontations between persons whose ways of life have no habitual or logical continuity with each other suggest the utmost incohesion in the stuff of experience.

Technique is vision. Dickens' technique is an index of a vision of life that sees human separatedness as the ordinary condition, where speech is speech *to* nobody and where human encounter is mere collision. But the vision goes much further. Our minds are so constituted that they insist on seeking in the use of language an exchange function, a delivery and a passing on of perceptions from soul to soul and generation to generation, binding them in some kind of order; and they insist on finding cause and effect, or *motivation*, in the displacements and encounters of persons or things. Without these primary patterns of perception we would not have what we call minds. And when these patterns are confused or abrogated by our experience, we are forced, in order to preserve some kind of psychic equilibrium, to seek them in extraordinary explanations—explanations again in terms of mutual exchange and cause and effect. Dickens saw his world patently all in pieces, and as a child's vision would offer some reasonable explanation of why such a world was that way—and, by the act of explanation, would make that world yield up a principle of order, however obscure or fantastic—so, with a child's literalism of imagination, he discovered organization among his fragments. . . .

THE RETURN OF MAGWITCH

What brings the convict Magwitch to the child Pip, in the graveyard, is more than the convict's hunger; Pip (or let us say simply "the child," for Pip is an Everyman) carries the convict inside him, as the negative potential of his "great expectations"—Magwitch is the concretion of his potential guilt. What brings Magwitch across the "great gulfs" of the Atlantic to Pip again, at the moment of revelation in the story, is their profoundly implicit compact of guilt, as binding as the convict's leg iron which is its recurrent symbol. The multiplying likenesses in the street as Magwitch draws nearer, coming over the sea, the mysterious warnings of his approach on the night of his reappearance, are moral pro-jections as "real" as the storm outside the windows and as the crouched form of the vicious Orlick on the dark stairs. The conception of what brings people together "coinciden-tally" in their seemingly uncaused encounters and collisions —the total change in the texture of experience that follows upon any act, public or private, external or in thought, the concreteness of the effect of the act not only upon the con-ceiving heart but upon the atoms of physical matter, so that blind nature collaborates daemonically in the drama of reprisal—is deep and valid in this book.

PSYCHOLOGICAL MONTAGE

In a finely lucid atmosphere of fairy tale, Dickens uses a kind of montage in *Great Expectations,* a superimposing of one image upon another with an immediate effect of hallu-cination, that is but one more way of representing his vision of a purely nervous and moral organization of reality. An in-stance is the scene in which Estella walks the casks in the old brewery. Estella's walking the casks is an enchanting rit-ual dance of childhood (like walking fence rails or railroad ties), but inexplicably present in the tableau is the suicidal figure of Miss Havisham hanging by her neck from a brew-ery beam. Accompanying each appearance of Estella—the star and the jewel of Pip's expectations—is a similarly dis-turbing ghost, an image of an unformed dread. When Pip thinks of her, though he is sitting in a warm room with a friend, he shudders as if in a wind from over the marshes. Her slender knitting fingers are suddenly horribly displaced by the marred wrists of a murderess. The technique of mon-tage is that of dreams, which know with awful precision the affinities between the guilt of our desires and the common-places of our immediate perceptions.

This device, of doubling one image over another, is paral-leled in the handling of character. In the sense that one im-plies the other, the glittering frosty girl Estella, and the de-cayed and false old woman, Miss Havisham, are not two characters but a single one, or a single essence with dual as-pects, as if composed by montage—a spiritual continuum, so to speak. For inevitably wrought into the fascinating jewel-likeness of Pip's great expectations, as represented by Es-tella, is the falsehood and degeneracy represented by Miss Havisham, the soilure on the unpurchased good. The boy

Pip and the criminal Magwitch form another such contin-uum. Magwitch, from a metaphysical point of view, is not outside Pip but inside him, and his apparition is that of Pip's own unwrought deeds: Pip, having adopted "great expecta-tions," will live by making people into Magwitches, into means for his ends. . . .

THE SINS OF THE FATHERS

Pip first becomes aware of the "identity of things" as he is held suspended heels over head by the convict; that is, in a world literally turned upside down. Thenceforth Pip's inte-rior landscape is inverted by his guilty knowledge of this man "who had been soaked in water, and smothered in mud, and lamed by stones, and cut by flints, and stung by nettles, and torn by briars." The apparition is that of all suf-fering that the earth can inflict, and that the apparition pre-sents itself to a child is as much as to say that every child, whatever his innocence, inherits guilt (as the potential of his acts) for the condition of man. The inversion of natural or-der begins here with first self-consciousness: the child is heir to the sins of the "fathers." Thus the crime that is always pervasive in the Dickens universe is identified in a new way—not primarily as that of the "father," nor as that of some public institution, but as that of the child—the original individual who must necessarily take upon himself respon-sibility for not only what is to be done in the present and the future, but what has been done in the past, inasmuch as the past is part and parcel of the present and the future. The child is the criminal, and it is for this reason that he is able to redeem his world; for the world's guilt is his guilt, and he can expiate it in his own acts.

The guilt of the child is realized on several levels. Pip ex-periences the psychological *form* (or feeling) of guilt before he is capable of voluntary evil; he is treated by adults—Mrs. Joe and Pumblechook and Wopsle—as if he were a felon, a young George Barnwell (a character in the play which Wopsle reads on the night when Mrs. Joe is attacked) want-ing only to murder his nearest relative, as George Barnwell murdered his uncle. This is the usual nightmare of the child in Dickens, a vision of imminent incarceration, fetters like sausages, lurid accusatory texts. He is treated, that is, as if he were a thing, manipulable by adults for the extraction of cer-tain sensations: by making him feel guilty and diminished, they are able to feel virtuous and great. But the psychological *form* of guilt acquires spiritual *content* when Pip himself conceives the tainted wish—the wish to be like the most powerful adult and to treat others as things. At the literal level, Pip's guilt is that of snobbery toward Joe Gargery, and snobbery is a denial of the human value of others. Symbolically, however, Pip's guilt is that of murder; for he steals the file with which the convict rids himself of his leg iron, and it is this leg iron, picked up on the marshes, with which Orlick attacks Mrs. Joe; so that the child does inevitably overtake his destiny, which was, like George Barnwell, to murder his nearest relative. But the "relative" whom Pip, adopting the venerable criminality of society, is, in the widest symbolic scope of intention, destined to murder is not Mrs. Joe but his "father," Magwitch—to murder in the socially chronic fashion of the Dickens world, which consists in the dehumanization of the weak, or in moral acquiescence to such murder. Pip is, after all, the ordinary mixed human being, one more Everyman in the long succession of them that literature has represented, but we see this Everyman as he develops from a child; and his destiny is directed by the ideals of his world—toward "great expectations" which involve the making of Magwitches—which involve, that is, murder. These are the possibilities that are projected in the opening scene of the book, when the young child, left with a burden on his soul, watches the convict limping off under an angry red sky, toward the black marshes, the gibbet, and the savage lair of the sea, in a still rotating landscape.

Love in *Great Expectations*

J. Hillis Miller

The eminent Dickens critic J. Hillis Miller, professor of literature at the University of California, Irvine, sees different kinds of love as the key to the moral meaning of *Great Expectations*. To grow morally, Pip must develop beyond the immature, selfish love he has felt for Estella and toward the mature, meaningful love he learns to feel for Magwitch in the novel's final third. When Pip and Estella are reunited at the book's end, the meaning of love is significantly changed for both of them, from a self-aggrandizing ideal to a self-sacrificing one.

For Dickens, as for the general tradition of ethical thought, love is the only successful escape from the unhappiness of singularity, the unhappiness of being this unique and isolated person, Pip.

For Dickens, as for generations of Christian moralists, love means sacrifice. Pip must abandon all the proud hopes which have formed the secret core of his life. He must abandon forever his project of being a gentleman, the belief that somewhere there is a place for him which he can possess by right. He must accept the fact that he can in no way transcend the gap between "the small bundle of shivers growing afraid of it all and beginning to cry" and the wind, sea, sky, and marshland, the alien universe—in no way, that is, but by willingly accepting this separation. And to accept this means to accept Magwitch, who springs up with "a terrible voice" from the marshes at the moment Pip becomes aware of his separateness.

Pip learns about love, then, not through Estella, but through the slow change in his relation to Magwitch. Only this change makes possible a transformation of his relation to Estella. Otherwise, Pip would have remained, even if he

Reprinted by permission of the publisher from *Charles Dickens: The World of His Novels*, by J. Hillis Miller, Cambridge, Mass.: Harvard University Press. Copyright © 1958 by the President and Fellows of Harvard College.

had possessed Estella, the submissive worshipper of a cold and distant authority. Just as Mrs. Joe atones for her cruelties to Pip and Joe by bowing down to Orlick, so Pip can escape from despair, from the total loss of his great expectations, only by a change in his attitude toward Magwitch. His acceptance of Magwitch is not only the relinquishment of his great expectations; it is also the replacement of these by a positive assertion that he, Pip alone, will be the source of the meaning of his own life. Pip finally accepts as the foundation of his life the guilt which has always haunted him: his secret and gratuitous act of charity to the escaped convict. Pip slowly realizes that if he betrays Magwitch . . . it will be to betray himself, to betray the possible foundation of himself by self-denial, by the abandonment of his egoistic expectations. And to betray Magwitch will be to plunge Magwitch back into the nothingness of the complete outcast. It is a case of the hunter hunted. Pip had been seeking in social position and in Estella a basis for his identity. Now he finds that he himself has been sought. . . . Pip has been seized, will-nilly, by Magwitch, and, whatever he does thenceforth, cannot avoid his tie to Magwitch. In Dickens' world, people exist in the exact degree that they exist in other people's eyes. And for Dickens, one person can impose on another, whether he wishes it or not, the responsibility of betraying him or being faithful to him. Pip attempts all through his life, until his change, to remain neutral toward Magwitch, to "beat the dust of Newgate out of his clothes," to wipe out of existence the charitable theft for Magwitch which happened so long ago in his childhood. But he cannot erase this act from existence. He can only betray it, or reaffirm it. His whole life has been determined by that initial act. In spite of himself Pip is forced into complicity with convicts. He is forced to make a choice: either give Magwitch up to the police, or commit against society the crime of harboring an escaped felon. . . .

PIP'S LOYALTY

But it is only slowly that Pip realizes what his faithfulness means. It means facing the fact that he and Magwitch are in the same position of isolation. If they do not help one another, no one will. It means discovering that each can help the other by offering himself as the foundation of the other's selfhood, Pip by sacrificing all his hopes, Magwitch by his change from a fierce desire to "make" a gentleman for revenge, to the de-

PIP AND HUCK FINN AND THEIR OUTLAW SPIRITUAL FATHERS

A remarkable similarity exists between Pip and Mark Twain's Huck Finn: Both boys form a bond with a criminal in the eyes of society—the convict Magwitch and the runaway slave Jim, respectively. Hana Wirth-Nesher points out that in both novels these outlaws and the boys' relationships with them become the key to the main characters' moral growth.

Pip and Huck are both initiated into their new lives by violating one of their society's precepts and, in doing so, acting morally without being aware of it. Each feels sinful and guilty about his action because his inconsequential status has led him to mistrust his intuition when it comes to moral matters. Pip filches a pie from his sister's pantry to feed a starving fugitive on Christmas Day; Huck helps another fugitive escape from his rightful owner. Each boy, while believing he sins in doing so, acts charitably toward a man who becomes the boy's spiritual father and is actually the vehicle of his moral awakening rather than of his moral downfall.

Hana Wirth-Nesher, "The Literary Orphan as National Hero: Huck and Pip," *Dickens Studies Annual*, 15 (1986), p. 262.

sire to help Pip be a gentleman for Pip's own sake: "For now my repugnance to him had all melted away, and in the hunted wounded shackled creature who held my hand in his, I only saw a man who had meant to be my benefactor, and who had felt affectionately, gratefully, and generously, towards me with great constancy through a series of years." Magwitch's handclasp, originally a symbolic appropriation of Pip as his creation and possession, now becomes the symbol of their mutual love, and of their willingness to sacrifice all for one another. This transformation is complete after the unsuccessful attempt to get Magwitch safely out of the country. Thereafter, Magwitch thinks only of Pip and not at all of the "society" he had so hated, and Pip thinks only of Magwitch.

Pip remains faithful to Magwitch, publicly manifesting his allegiance throughout Magwitch's imprisonment, trial, and death. He hides from Magwitch the fact that all his money will be forfeited to the crown, and that his hopes of leaving Pip a gentleman will fail. And just before Magwitch dies Pip tells him that Estella, his child, is still alive, "is a lady and very beautiful. And I love her!" This is in a way his greatest sacrifice. He admits that he even owes Estella to Magwitch, and brings all the hope and dreams which had centered on Estella completely into the orbit of his relation to Magwitch. Magwitch is the source of everything he has and is.

By choosing his servitude to Magwitch, Pip transforms it into freedom. . . . No character in Dickens finally achieves authentic selfhood by establishing direct relation to God. Only the mutually self-denying, self-creating relationship of love succeeds, whereas the active assertion of will and the passive hope of great expectations both fail.

The divine power functions in *Great Expectations* primarily as the supreme judge before whom all social distinctions are as nothing: "The sun was striking in at the great windows of the court, through the glittering drops of rain upon the glass, and it made a broad shaft of light between the two-and-thirty [criminals] and the Judge, linking both together, and perhaps reminding some among the audience, how both were passing on, with absolute equality, to the greater Judgment that knoweth all things and cannot err." There is a true religious motif here. The light is God's judgment before which earthly judge and earthly judged, gentleman and common thief, are equal. But the meaning of the passage is as much social as religious. It is a final dramatization of the fact that social eminence such as Pip had sought and social judgments such as have hounded Magwitch all his life are altogether unimportant as sources of selfhood. At the center of Dickens' novels is a recognition of the bankruptcy of the relation of the individual to society as it now exists, the objective structure of given institutions and values. Only what an individual makes of himself, in charitable relations to others, counts. And this self-creation tends to require open revolt against the pressures of society. Human beings are themselves the source of the transcendence of their isolation.

Once Pip has established his new relationship to Magwitch he is able at last to win Estella. Pip's final love for Estella is a single complex relation which is both identification with the loved person (he is no longer conscious of a lack, a void of unfulfilled desire), and separation (he is still aware of himself as a self, as a separate identity; he does not melt into the loved person, and lose himself altogether). . . .

LOVE TRANSFORMED

Pip and Estella have experienced before their union their most complete separation, Pip in the agony of his discovery that Estella is not destined for him and that Magwitch is his real benefactor, and Estella in her unhappy marriage to Bentley Drummle, who has "used her with great cruelty," just as Pip has been "used" by Estella. These experiences have transformed them both. It is only when Estella has been tamed by the cruelty of her bad husband that she and Pip can enter into a wholly different relationship. Only when Estella's proud, cold glance is transformed into "the saddened softened light of the once proud eyes" can she and Pip transform the fettering of slave by master into the handclasp of love. Estella too must suffer the slave's loss of selfhood in order to be herself transformed. Both have come back from a kind of death to meet and join in the moonlight in Miss Havisham's ruined garden. . . . Estella and Pip are accepting their exile from the garden of false hopes. Now that the mists of infatuation have cleared away Pip and Estella are different persons. They go forth from the ruined garden into a fallen world. In this world their lives will be given meaning only by their own acts and by their dependence on one another. Pip now has all that he wanted, Estella and her jewels, but what he has is altogether different from what he expected. Rather than possessing the impossible reconciliation of freedom and security he had sought in Estella and in gentility, he now loves and is loved by another fallible and imperfect being like himself:

> The silvery mist was touched with the first rays of the moonlight, and the same rays touched the tears that dropped from her eyes. . . .

> I took her hand in mine, and we went out of the ruined place; and, as the morning mists had risen long ago when I first left the forge, so, the evening mists were rising now, and in all the broad expanse of tranquil light they showed to me, I saw no shadow of another parting from her.

A Negative Commentary on Victorian Society

Allan Grant

In *Great Expectations,* Dickens characterizes society negatively, according to Allan Grant, late professor of humanities at the University of London. He begins his unfavorable portrayal with the oppressive Christmas dinner at the Gargerys and continues with the grotesque spectacle of decay and death at Satis House, where Pip learns to hate himself and believe in illusions. The City of London is typified by the bullying of Jaggers and the ugliness of his office and his work. Finally, Pip's snobbery toward Joe in London shows not only his own, but society's, capacity for callousness and inhumanity. What Pip ultimately learns from his experience with society, according to Grant, is that "personal survival lies not in seeking its approval or in embracing it, but in escaping it." Put another way, Pip's self-loathing for being a full-fledged member of a cruel, dysfunctional society eventually forces him to renounce his membership in it altogether.

What kind of society is it that Dickens evokes in the novel and towards which Pip aspires? What are the growing individual's relations with it? We begin to glimpse something of the answers to such questions in the chilly comedy of the family Christmas dinner which, even without the secret terror of his encounters with the convict on the marshes, was an occasion of misery for the child. Then later, as he moves beyond the confines of the forge and the marshes, he is overcome by the utter strangeness of Miss Havisham and her surroundings. Pip reports everything he sees at Satis House, including his hallucinated vision of Miss Havisham hanging

Excerpted from *A Preface to Dickens* by Allan Grant. Copyright © 1984 Longman Group Ltd. Reprinted by permission of Addison Wesley Longman Ltd.

from a beam high up in the long-neglected brewery. But in doing so, he fails to make for himself the obvious inference that it is a world fixed in the past and everywhere in decay; a world of death. He is drawn towards this world by the accidental collision with the pantomimic pale young gentleman with whom he fights and whom he knocks down. That, on this occasion, he should feel 'but a gloomy satisfaction' in his victory and think of himself as a 'savage young wolf' (one recalls the phrase when, in the sluice-house later, Orlick also calls him 'wolf' and 'young wolf') shows vividly to what extent he has already come to share society's view of that self. Further, that Estella, whom the fight had excited, should offer her cheek for him to kiss as a reward ensured that he will continue to be attracted towards her if only because the kiss inflames his feeling of worthlessness beside her. By this point in his progress his education in guilt and shame is complete. To escape them he takes the route that society approves.

NEW CLOTHES FOR A DIRTY CITY

The immediate response to the announcement of his great expectations is Pumblechook's 'May I? *may* I?' which is splendid fun as a display of self-abasing ingratiation that Pip, to his credit, finds intolerable. It perplexes him that Trabb, the tailor, must also take new measurements for his grand new clothes, since he already has them, but he is assured that, 'it wouldn't do under existing circumstances, sir—it wouldn't do at all'. It is as though Pip must be made to see that he is already a different person.

Wearing his new clothes, he pays a last call on Miss Havisham whom he twice refers to as his 'fairy-godmother'. It is as though Dickens wants to emphasise the illusion that Pip is swayed by; Jaggers spoke only of an unknown benefactor. Miss Havisham, however, uses the occasion for her own ends by allowing her cousin Sarah Pocket, who is present as an agent of a family anxious to inherit Miss Havisham's wealth, to infer that she is in fact Pip's benefactor. Pip takes it that his wild fancy has been confirmed, thus rendering unbearable to him his ultimate disillusionment.

However, it is only once Pip has established himself in London that the reader is invited to take the full measure of the society of wealth and status for which Pip is being educated. His first impression of the place is both that its immensity was scaring and that it was 'rather ugly, crooked, narrow and dirty'. Mr Jaggers's office is located at its very heart in Little Britain. The street was a real street in Dickens's time which still exists, but one cannot help but admire the ironic, if unforced, appropriateness of the name to Dickens's subject. In close proximity lie huddled together St Paul's Cathedral, Newgate Prison, and Smithfield Market. Again, the juxtaposition is unforced and geographically accurate but it makes a powerful comment on society's arrangements. The first object he is shown is the gallows yard in the prison and the Debtors' Door and is given to understand that 'four on 'em would come out at that door the day after tomorrow at eight in the morning, to be killed in a row'. The site and the explanation give him a 'sickening idea of London'.

Jaggers's office is no better: his black horse-hair chair is like a coffin and the casts of two swollen faces on a shelf are those of clients who were hanged. When Pip finally sees Jaggers, the lawyer is surrounded by clients and supplicants whom he terrifies, just as his name had terrified Pip's coachman into accepting the correct fare. Jaggers dominates Pip's experience of London. He is all-powerful in the law, manipulating and bullying it as he chooses or as he is paid. The whole world, as it seems, is frightened of him and he even bullies his lunch-time sandwich. Yet he wields his power utterly irresponsibly. When he goes home he washes his hands carefully in scented soap and is free of any connection with his office world, although he seems to inhabit no other nor to possess a private life nor a private self. As Pip's guardian, he refuses all personal responsibility, remarking only of the arrangements made on Pip's behalf 'of course you'll go wrong somehow, but that's no fault of mine'. That his private nature coheres almost entirely with his professional character is made clear on the occasion in chapter twenty-six of the invitation to Pip and his friends to dine with him at home. In a telling gesture, he scrapes his work out of his nails with his penknife and, after bluntly telling his guests to go, retires once again behind a clean towel to wash his hands of them. During the dinner itself, he takes particular note of the most disagreeable of Pip's companions, expertly raises a disagreement and a contest of physical strength among them and ends it by forcing his housekeeper to display her scarred, powerful wrists.

The dinner is not only a confirmation of what the reader has already been directed towards in the character of Jaggers but, at the same time, one in a series of meals in this novel that are eaten without enjoyment, without genuine hospitality or any expression of the warmth of human relationship. The most significant of these is the untouched wedding feast which has lain for years spread on the large table at Satis House, serving only spiders and mice with nourishment. Jaggers's idea of hospitality contrasts totally and comically with that of his clerk, Wemmick. Pip's first impression of Wemmick is that, with his pillar-box mouth and his general demeanour at the office, he is of the same, closed kind as his employer. Yet like Pip, he was new to London once, and has taken on a professional protective disguise. Wemmick survives the world of London by having perfected a total separation of his social and private selves. He is twins in effect, and Pip soon meets and comes to recognise the hidden, Walworth twin. At home in Walworth, life is full of spontaneous warmth of feeling and ingenious playfulness that has transformed a cottage in a garden plot into a bower and a defended castle with moat and drawbridge. It is as though in the description Dickens is enjoying an extended pun on the meanings of the word 'retreat'. 'So, sir . . . if you can suppose the little place besieged, it would hold out a devil of a time . . .' Wemmick's private world is full of fantasy but it is a fantasy of siege conditions, the house is in need of defence, against presumably, the encroachments of the outer social world which seems to Wemmick to threaten his private world of family and feasting. Even that most social of ceremonies, his wedding, in which the private and public selves appear as one, must be conducted surreptitiously in a denial of its public and social aspects. To Pip's surprise, Mr Jaggers has never seen Walworth to admire it. 'No; the office is one thing, and private life is another. When I go into the office, I leave the Castle behind me, and when I come into the Castle, I leave the office behind me. If it's not in any way disagreeable to you, you'll oblige me by doing the same. I don't wish it professionally spoken about.' At the office it is as though the gaiety and ceremony of the Walworth Castle had never existed. The constraints under which Wemmick serves Jaggers appear again as he accompanies Pip back across the river to his place of business. 'By degrees, Wemmick got dryer and harder as we went along, and his mouth tightened into a post-office again.'

PIP'S LONDON ASSOCIATES

The remainder of Pip's circle of acquaintance in London is narrowly circumscribed. It consists of the Pocket family and the small group of young men who like himself have come to study with Mr Matthew Pocket, a 'serious, honest and good' man always 'zealous and honourable' as Pip reports. Mrs Pocket, on the other hand, carries through life a conviction that she should have been a duchess. The fixation on the aristocracy for which she has failed to qualify by marriage excuses her any responsibility for the domestic arrangements. Her children are therefore 'tumbled up' by an assortment of incompetent servants whom Mr Pocket can scarcely afford. His goodness and seriousness disqualify him from the rewards of success and status which society of offers. The same may be said of his son Herbert, the pale young gentleman of the childhood boxing match, who is now to be Pip's companion and social mentor. At the very beginning of their friendship Pip twice records an odd impression he has that Herbert, for all his 'looking about' for a future in shipping insurance, will never be successful or rich.

Nevertheless, Herbert and his father are gentlemen and Herbert's induction of Pip into his new role in society is gentle, humouring and quite free of jealousy. Pip feels that Herbert also knows the source of his fortune, but that he has been put at ease on the subject since Herbert, despite the relative poverty of his father, displays nothing of the remainder of the family's assiduous toadying to Miss Havisham. Furthermore, Dickens gives us through the mouth of Herbert a disquisition on the qualities of the gentleman. According to Herbert it is a principle of his father's that 'no man who was not a true gentleman at heart, ever was, since the world began, a true gentleman in manner. He says no varnish can hide the grain of the wood; and that the more varnish you put on, the more the grain will express itself.' Without appearing to break the dramatic surface of the writing in this novel, Dickens is at times surprisingly direct in his address to the reader. It is clear from the passage that Dickens is giving assent to the idea of a gentleman that Herbert expresses. At the same time it is made equally clear that to be a gentleman and to be socially successful are incompatible ambitions. It is part of Pip's better nature that he feels his deficiencies in a way that makes him stick to his studies. His better nature is also supported by his friendship with Herbert and with the Walworth side of Wemmick, but these friendships are not enough to prevent his sliding into debt, dissipation and a life composed of trivialities in the company of a club called the Finches of the Grove. The Finches, apart from his fellow private students, remain anonymous, but confirm for the reader a sense of the aimlessness of the way of life of the set of wealthy young men.

CHOOSING ESTELLA OVER JOE

During this period of Pip's young life, it is the interruption to his nullifying routine that demands our attention. It is, after all, a lull, a period of waiting until the moment when his benefactor should reveal his identity. First, there is the visit from Joe announced in Biddy's respectful letter. That it is not a success is the result of Pip's inability to break through Joe's notion of the deference due to gentility. Pip would rather his old friend and play-mate had not come at all and, despite feeling remorseful about it, is greatly relieved to see the back of him. The visit is punctuated by the refusal of Joe's hat to remain on the mantelpiece where he felt obliged to put it. The comedy with the hat is a sign of the unnatural constraint that Pip imposes on the situation by his unwillingness to relax. Between them, Joe and Pip perform an unmanageable balancing act and have difficulty in maintaining the roles they have forced upon themselves. It was Pip's place to accept Joe for what he was, not for what Joe, in the awkwardness of his novel situation, thought was required of him. After Joe's departure, Pip hesitates before going down to call him back, long enough for Joe to have disappeared. Pip's confession of his hesitation recalls that similar delay he reports to us earlier of wishing to get down from the coach that first carried him away from Joe and the forge towards London and his new life of great expectations. He delays long enough to make a return impossible. On each occasion one can see a very different kind of explanation for the delay from the one Pip offers. He it is who breaks away; Joe merely releases him and will accept no compensation for the loss of his apprentice.

More in tune at this time with the ambitions he nurses are Pip's resumed relations with Estella, whom, in his own words, he has fastened to the innermost life of his life. It is on the coach journey to see her again at Miss Havisham's that he is forcefully reminded of what he is trying to escape by fastening his dreams to Estella, when the convict breathing down his neck on top of the coach provokes in him a vague and undefined fear that he describes as the revival of the terror of childhood. It is the central irony in the novel that the harder he attempted to suppress his original guilt and shame of which his undefined terror is the symptom, the nearer he comes to being forced to acknowledge them. Estella plays an important role in the socially approved life that Pip thinks he is making for himself when, all the while, she is a convict's daughter and, like Pip, the instrument of another's desire for revenge on that society.

SOCIETY'S THREAT

The society from which Pip seeks approval is revealed as one in which power derives from status and wealth where the possession of either of these distinctions divided man from man. Personal survival lies not in seeking its approval or in embracing it, but in escaping it. Pip's liberation from the miseries of his past comes not from society nor from his fantasy of a destined life with Estella in a restored Satis House, but from those past experiences which he has striven most to keep hidden: the earliest sources of his feelings of guilt and shame. Like Pip, who hides things from the reader and from himself, society hides much and represses more. In the telling gesture of its most powerful representative, Jaggers, it washes its hands of human responsibility and of all that relates human beings to each other.

CHAPTER 2

Symbols and Structure in *Great Expectations*

Relationships and Their Meaning

William F. Axton

William F. Axton, professor of English at the University of Louisville, examines the patron/protégé relationships between Magwitch and Pip and between Miss Havisham and Estella. Axton argues that the superior patron provides for the inferior protégé in order to use this person as a tool or object for the patron's private purposes, such as revenge. Dickens contrasts these relationships with nonexploitive relationships—such as Joe's relationships with Biddy and Pip, and Herbert Pocket's relationships with Clara and Pip—in which, Axton claims, there is "friendship that transcends self-interest . . . love that has no other end in view than the welfare of the beloved." Axton points out that Pip confuses genuine friendship with the self-serving patron/protégé relationship. His moral confusion is apparent when he tries to make protégés of Biddy and Joe, and of Herbert Pocket as well; he does this to feel better about himself. Pip's moral regeneration in the final third of the novel begins only when he recognizes the exploitative nature of this type of relationship. It is finally achieved through the transformation of his relationships with others from unions of manipulation and fear to unions of humility and love.

Having "great expectations" enters the novel as the generative principle of wrongdoing, but "great expectations" considered not only as wealth, leisure, or social position, but more importantly and pervasively in the sense of asking more from life than, under the limitations imposed by one's nature, station, or the general conditions of existence, it can reasonably be expected to return. The habit of holding great, but unreal-

Excerpted from *"Great Expectations* Yet Again," by William F. Axton, *Dickens Studies Annual*, vol. 2, 1972, pp. 278–93. Reproduced by arrangement with AMS Press, Inc., New York.

istic or unobtainable expectations of life is the source of wrong, evil, and finally of guilt in *Great Expectations*. This is so because those whose expectations have been thwarted commonly turn out of a sense of injustice, to revenge; but this vengeance is directed toward or through the innocent. Or else, those who entertain great expectations are led into condescension, irresponsibility, patronage, timeserving, ingratitude, or the imputation of evil to others. At the heart of these themes and their source is the patron-protégé relationship, a type of the much more fundamental theme of instrumentality—that is, the tendency to create relationships between people based on an interchange of patronage and dependency, superiority and inferiority, *noblesse oblige*, and extorted gratitude, in which each party "expects" something in return that will serve the self. Every human relationship is cankered by its exploitation as an instrument of self-aggrandizement—love, friendship, parenthood, and other ties of blood, even benevolence: indeed, it is the expectation of getting something for oneself out of a relationship with another which is finally the source of evil in *Great Expectations*, whether that "something" be revenge, wealth, status, moral ascendency, sadistic pleasure, a sense of superiority, extorted gratitude, or mere condescension. In contrast, an alternative system of radically egalitarian values centered on Joe Gargery, Biddy, and Trabb's boy argues the moral preferability of a mutually disinterested interchange of love and affection as the basis for human relationships, one altogether indifferent to class distinctions and personal advantage or disadvantage, one which substitutes love and affection for hatred or obsessive infatuation, forgiveness for revenge, friendship for patronage, and responsibility for that imputation of evil to others which clears one's own skirts. The essential character of wrongdoing in this novel therefore consists in the betrayal or denial of humane relationship by an inhumane one; and events bring the traitor at last to a realization of his wrong and to forgiveness. . . .

A FRAUDULENT ASSUMPTION

The novel's comic epitome of the system of values which supposes that relationships between people are based on a mutually accepted hierarchy of patrons and protégés, equally self-serving to both parties in the bargain, is that egregious hypocrite, Pumblechook, who alternately bullies the boy Pip when a mere blacksmith's apprentice, fawns before the new-made gentleman, and arrogates to himself the role of patron, and later, that of neglected benefactor. The fraudulent assumption of the distance imposed by largesse and gratitude, superiority and abasement, is the operative principle; its upshot is injustice.

The notion that wealth and position determine the essential quality of people is countered by a strain of radical egalitarianism in the novel most pointedly represented by the audacious figure of Trabb's boy, who steadfastly refuses to acknowledge Pip's rise in station as in any way imposing a distance between them, who satirizes Pip's attempts to gain a moral ascendancy over him by his gentlemanly clothes and manner, and who finally affirms their common citizenship in the republic of mankind by saving Pip's life.

Pip's wrongdoing, similarly, consists in trying to make Joe and Biddy protégés to his patronage and, when they resist, to condemn them for faults which are really his own. In either case, the methods are interoperative: the assertion of superiority implies an imputation of inferiority both social and moral that is self-aggrandizing to the aggressor. The aim remains irresponsible; it is to clear one's skirts of any personal involvement with one's fellow-men. . . .

That caste, rank, and status, whether conferred by blood relationship, as in the case of Matthew Pocket's wife, Belinda, or by money, as in the case of Pip and Estella, are centrally involved in the novel's complex scheme of injustice, irresponsibility, neglect and exploitation, and revenge which together comprise the constituent elements of its themes, seems indisputable. We have seen how neglect and exploitation by an entire social structure create a criminal class which the criminal code then condemns and punishes, a process perilously close to the psychology of Orlick and the other vengeance-minded characters in this novel. Belinda Pocket, on the other hand, displays a different side of the same coin. She is a leading instance of the manner in which pride of place—her father, a Knight, suffered from the delusion that he had unjustly missed becoming a Baronet—results in neglect of those dependent upon her—children, husband, household. Absorbed in unreal reveries about her near approach to nobility, she ignores her responsibilities as wife, mother, and mistress of her house and condescends to those around her, in particular her impecunious husband,

Matthew. Thus Mrs. Pocket picks up the strand introduced by Mrs. Joe, just as Mr. Pocket does of Joe: both husbands are victims of women who feel that they have married beneath themselves and who either take vengeance on their dependents or neglect and exploit them, out of motives prompted by a wounded sense of superior status, injustice, or frustrated expectations.

Miss Havisham is again at the heart of this theme, and not alone through her blood relationship to the Pocket family. As Herbert Pocket relates her story to Pip on their first evening at Barnard's Inn, she was the spoiled daughter of a brewer who had succeeded in achieving genteel status—"I don't know why it should be a crack thing to be a brewer; but it is indisputable that while you cannot possibly be genteel and bake, you may be as genteel as never was and brew. You see it every day'." Having lost her mother in childhood and her father in early womanhood, she reaches maturity a proud, self-willed heiress, prey to any fortune hunter. It is then that the adventurer, Compeyson, enters the story at the behest of her half brother, Arthur, her father's son by a secret second marriage to his cook. Upon the latter's death, the son was recognized and introduced into Satis House. But because of his profligacy, Arthur was cut off by his father's will with only a very small share of the family estate, and in consequence "he cherished a deep and mortal grudge" against Miss Havisham for having turned his father against him. As Orlick determines to revenge himself on Pip, whom he conceived to be unjustly standing in his way at the forge, so Arthur Havisham employs Compeyson to gain vengeance against his half sister who was unjustly preferred at Satis House. Using Compeyson to capture his sister's heart, he may then gain control over her fortune and proceed to fleece her, saving the most exquisite part of his revenge for last, when her paramour throws her over on the wedding morning. The "gentleman" uses a "gentleman" to gain revenge on the one whom he blames for a frustration of his expectations that was in fact the consequence of his own vice.

The betrayal of the young heiress, as everyone knows, turns her into a morbid recluse who gradually warps her adopted daughter Estella into an instrument of revenge against the male sex, in the course of which Pip becomes tragically involved. By making Estella into an object of Pip's idolatrous infatuation, like that which Miss Havisham felt for Compeyson, and by encouraging the young man in his erroneous belief that he is Miss Havisham's protégé, secretly elevated to genteel status in order to make him a suitable partner for the celestial Estella, her revenge consists in raising expectations that must be frustrated. The cruelty that she practices upon Pip is only partially motivated by her desire to revenge herself on the male sex. In part she fosters the illusion of Pip's favor in her eyes in order to torture and frustrate the expectations of her timeserving cousins, Sarah and Camilla Pocket, who dance attendance on her in hopes of sharing largely in her fortune upon her death. Miss Havisham's primary scheme of revenge miscarries in part because Estella comes to hate the self that her foster-mother has made of her and, in perverse revenge upon the woman who has warped her, throws herself away in a masochistic union with the stupid and brutal Bentley Drummle. In part, however, Miss Havisham herself comes to realize and feel remorse for the wreckage she had made of two innocent lives in her keeping, and on her deathbed pleads for forgiveness. The reading of her will, on the other hand, is a triumphant consummation of her scheme of vengeance against her hypocritical Pocket cousins, Sarah and Camilla, who are cut off with a pittance. At the same time, her loyal and disinterested cousin, Matthew Pocket, who alone among her relatives had penetrated the gentlemanly façade of Compeyson and warned her against putting herself so completely in his power—with the result that she turned him out of the house—is rewarded with a handsome legacy. In thus practicing on the greed, envy, and hypocrisy of her cousins, Miss Havisham takes her revenge for having been victimized by Compeyson and yet does justice in the process.

Miss Havisham's life following her abandonment by Compeyson is framed to hide from herself her own fault in the affair, in part by morbidly embracing the condition of a recluse, in part by casting the blame for her unhappiness on to the male sex. Indeed, her principal motivation for withdrawing behind the walls of Satis House and laying it waste seems to have been humiliation, not guilt: having prostrated herself wholly before her lover and having been brought low by his abandonment, she abandons herself to self-pity and vengeance. In this she is a counterpart of Mrs. Joe.

Again, like Mrs. Joe, she expects or extorts gratitude from those to whom she serves as foster-mother, from those who hope to share in her bounty, or who believe that they already do—respectively Estella, Sarah and Camilla Pocket, and Pip. Yet neither Miss Havisham nor Mrs. Joe can find this gratitude in those who have been exploited as instruments of their revenge. Mrs. Joe never receives from Pip the love or sense of indebtedness which he freely gives, because it is unasked, to Joe; and Miss Havisham comes at last to recognize the hatred Estella feels toward her for having made her into a creature incapable of love or gratitude.

"FRIENDSHIP THAT TRANSCENDS SELF-INTEREST"

But the chain of injustice, vengeance, extorted gratitude, and evaded responsibility is broken significantly when those who have used others for their own twisted purposes come to realize the enormity of their wrong and beg forgiveness of their victims, as Mrs. Joe does on the morning of her death with the broken "Joe . . . Pardon . . . Pip," as Miss Havisham does when she enjoins Pip to "take the pencil and write under my name, 'I forgive her,'" and as Pip does following the illness through which Joe nursed him. Moreover, both Pip and Estella must be brought by suffering to understand their own wrongdoing and seek forgiveness from those who were the victims of their injustice. In Estella's case, the victim is Pip, whom she tormented while he loved her and betrayed by marrying Bentley Drummle.

> You said to me [once before] . . . "God bless you, God forgive you!" And if you could say that to me then, you will not hesitate to say that to me now—now, when suffering has been stronger than all other teaching, and has taught me to understand what your heart used to be.

With this, the novel's long circle of injustice, revenge, and forgiveness comes round upon itself.

At the core of this latter theme stands the patron-protégé relationship, inasmuch as it engages the themes of gratitude and thanklessness, obligation and irresponsibility, love and infatuation, gentility and gentleness. *Great Expectations* abounds in patrons and protégés of every shape and description, all eager to use this relationship to gain something for themselves: fraudulent ones like Pumblechook, genuine ones like Magwitch, who began in simple gratitude to the boy who once helped him, and those somewhere in between, like Miss Havisham and Mrs. Joe, who are alternately a little of both.

What poisons this relationship is that it is never assumed disinterestedly: it plays upon and perpetuates a system of values that subverts human ones; it exploits or corrupts its recipients; it extorts gratitude from or imputes blame to its victims; and it thrives on and encourages not obligation but irresponsibility, not love but ambition or vengeance, not fulfillment but frustration, not equality but degree and distance, not equity but injustice.

In contrast stand the novel's many instances of genuine and disinterested responsibility for others, like that of Wemmick for his "Aged P"; of friendship that transcends self-interest, like that of Herbert Pocket for Pip; of love that has no other end in view but the welfare of the beloved, like that of Pocket for Clara Barley, of Biddy for Joe, and of Joe for Pip, and hence finds it easy to forgive transgressions because there is nothing to revenge; even, finally, of patronage that conceals itself, like that of Pip toward Pocket. These relationships are unique in the novel in that they are wholly lacking in any instrumental character: they exist for their intrinsic value alone and not as means to some other, selfish end. They have, in short, no great expectations but those of justice. Thus, where other relationships further revenge for wrongs done by another, these forgive and forget; where others impute evil, these compassionate; where others plume the self, these are anonymous and undemanding; where others exploit, neglect, betray, or abandon, these are loyal and responsible; where others promote the differences of rank and status, these level all to a common moral egalitarianism based on simple gentleness; where others are passionate, obsessed, or infatuated, these are calm, deep, and abiding.

These themes finally precipitate into a single issue, the question of love, and particularly love as it engages the relationship between the self and others, between the lover and the beloved; for the moral tenor of this relationship is determined by the maintenance of the equality, integrity, and identity of the partners: their justice toward one another. The canker at the heart of the emotional relationships in *Great Expectations*, as of its moral and social relationships, is distance and degree, but expressed in this context in terms of domination and abasement—and therefore of justice—self-respect and respect for one's beloved. Once again, Miss Havisham and Magwitch give the key and set the tone for everything else, since each conceives of love or affection in terms of self-abasement. Miss Havisham's morbid conception of love—"blind devotion, unquestioning self-humiliation, utter submission, trust and belief against yourself and against the whole world, giving up your whole heart and soul to the smiter—as I did!"—she communicates to Pip, who as we have already seen prostrates himself before his vision of Estella. Estella, on the other hand, is sufficiently perverse to subject herself to the tender mercies of marriage with Drummle. Through their different but analogous sufferings, both Pip and Estella win through to a human love relationship based upon an equitable interchange of compassionate understanding. Magwitch, meanwhile, while loving his manufactured gentleman, abases himself before Pip because of his "lowness"; indeed, Pip's moral regeneration consists in transcending his patron's sense of inferiority by affirming their equality. Similarly, it was Pip's earlier subversion of the affectionate commonwealth that had existed between him, Joe, and Biddy in the days at the forge which constitutes the substantial wrong he does as a would-be gentleman. It is this very moral identity that Biddy asserts, much to Pip's discomfiture, in the two scenes between them following the young man's "rise in fortune"; and it is the barrier imposed between Joe and Pip by the latter's consciousness of his superior station that denies the equivalence implied by Joe's oft-repeated "Ever the best of friends, Pip!" For what is wrong with love relationships which involve abasement of one partner or the other is, paradoxically, that the act of humiliation carries with it a claim for possession: to be possessed as Pip and Miss Havisham are is to seek to possess, as Pip, Miss Havisham, and Magwitch do in their various ways. This theme accounts for the existence of Jaggers' housekeeper, the tigress Molly, Magwitch's sometime common-law wife and Estella's natural mother, a savage murderess who killed in a paroxysm of possessive jealousy. In contrast, the reader is asked to attend to the gentle and undemanding love of Pocket for Clara Barley and of Joe and Biddy—even their comic counterpart in the persons of Wemmick and Miss Skiffins. By refraining from the desire to possess another, they avoid both possession and being possessed. The principal moral irony of *Great Expectations*, then, is that these gain the only things of any value. Put another way, it consists in the allegation that gentility means gentleness, wherever it is found; and that the latter means justice, equity.

The Importance of Place

Taylor Stoehr

Taylor Stoehr, an English professor at Cornell University, analyzes the structure of *Great Expectations* by examining the various locations in the novel. Stoehr argues that places in the novel are symbolic. For example, the novel begins with a conflict between the domestic world of the forge (Joe and Mrs. Joe) and the criminal world of the marshes (Magwitch and Compeyson). It then shifts to a conflict between the lower-class world of the forge and the upper-class world of Satis House (Miss Havisham and Estella). In London, in the second part of the novel, the conflict is between Pip's ambitions and his secret past, represented by Newgate Prison. When Magwitch returns to London, the conflict begins to be resolved as Pip recognizes that Newgate Prison and Magwitch are what is real for him, not Satis House and Estella. These places—the forge, the marshes, Satis House, and Newgate Prison—represent Pip's hopes and fears, his pride and shame.

In Dickens place has an organizing function beyond that of mere background. There are two main strands of action in *Great Expectations*: one concerned with Pip's relations to Miss Havisham and Estella and their symbolic place of residence, Satis House; the other centered around the transported felon Abel Magwitch and his symbolic place, Newgate prison. These two strains, filtered through Pip's consciousness, not only give us the content of his life (the events that occur, the people he meets), but also reflect in their emotional tone the inner conflict of his character, which is the central dilemma of the novel. A third set of characters, Joe and Biddy, and their symbolic place, the

Forge, seems at the beginning to furnish the major alternative to the world of Satis House, and through the first third of the novel the conflict seems to be between these two worlds alone; but after Pip's departure for London the Forge fades out of the picture, and Newgate takes its place in opposition to Satis House.

The conflict between the worlds of Newgate (or the Forge) and Satis House is a conflict in Pip's soul. Thus it is given in the structure of the novel as the working out of his conflicting interpretations of the things that happen to him, which are the events of the novel itself. Pip's expectations may derive, as he first supposes, from Miss Havisham, because she has taken a fancy to him; or their source may be, as he finally discovers, the convict Magwitch, grateful for Pip's childhood kindness to him on the marshes. Each possibility has full-fledged formal status, in that it involves a set of characters and incidents structurally interrelated. . . . The Havisham strand fills the surface of the narrative, while the Magwitch strand lies mysteriously in the background, seemingly unrelated to the progress of the action. In the opening episode (Chapters I to VI), Magwitch jerks Pip up bodily and symbolically into the hidden strand, when, in a scene that is nightmarish in its blend of comedy and terror, he turns him upside down to shake his pockets empty. But Pip has not yet rejected the Forge, and Magwitch fades into the background while the narrative chiefly recounts Pip's fall from grace, his growing bedazzlement with the mirage of Satis House (begun in Chapter VII). Regularly interspersed, however, are incidents which stem, as even Pip can see, from the first scenes with the convict on the marshes. Thus in Chapter X, Pip meets a stranger who stirs his rum-and-water with Joe's stolen file and gives Pip a shilling wrapped up in a pair of pound notes—a gift from Magwitch. That night, in Pip's guilty slumbers,

> I saw the file coming at me out of a door, without seeing who held it, and I screamed myself awake.

Following a few more scenes with Miss Havisham, Chapter XV deals with two more convicts escaped from the hulks, and with an act of violence for which Pip feels partly responsible—the savage attack on Mrs. Joe. As Pip says at the beginning of Chapter XVI,

> With my head full of George Barnwell [an amateur reading had been forced on Pip by the stage-struck Wopsle], I was at

first disposed to believe that *I* must have had some hand in
the attack upon my sister, or at all events that as her near relation, popularly known to be under obligations to her, I was
a more legitimate object of suspicion than any one else.

Pip conjectures that "either Orlick, or the strange man who
had shown me the file" is the culprit. He knows that he himself was the cause of a violent squabble that very day between his sister and Orlick; and, worst of all, Mrs. Joe was
beaten with a convict's iron—the very one that Pip had
watched Magwitch file from his leg years before:

> It was horrible to think that I had provided the weapon, how-
> ever undesignedly, but I could hardly think otherwise.

Thus, mingling with Pip's swelling ambitions are his growing feelings of guilt; Magwitch and the Newgate strand are
slowly beginning to replace the Forge and to present an alternative version of the facts as Pip sees them, although he
cannot yet recognize this alternative.

Perhaps there is little need to emphasize the dreamlike
cast of places and events in this opening sequence. Critics
have often drawn attention to it, especially to the bizarre ex-
travagance of the scenes laid at Satis House. It may be worth
pointing out, however, that the carefully paced glimpses we
have of the Newgate strand depend heavily for their threat-
ening power on this eerie quality—which so pervades the atmosphere whenever the Magwitch cluster reappears that
Pip's dream of "the file coming at me out of a door" seems
hardly hallucinated at all. Compare it, for example, with the
immediately preceding encounter with the convict who stirs
his rum-and-water with that same file. And Pip later says
that the two pound notes the convict had given him,
"sealed . . . [by Mrs. Joe] in a piece of paper, and put . . . under some dried rose-leaves in an ornamental tea-pot, . . . remained a nightmare to me many and many a night and
day.". . .

FROM SATIS HOUSE TO LONDON

"The Second Stage of Pip's Expectations" takes place in London, where the Newgate strand completely supplants that of
the Forge. Pip is now entirely in the throes of moral conflict.
At one moment he is full of vanity and self-importance, hir-
ing a servant, joining the Finches of the Grove, sinking himself and Herbert into debt, and generally behaving like a
"gentleman"; in the next, he is guiltily brooding over his past

associations with convicts and other "low" persons, Joe included. His single good act comes when he secretly provides the money to make Herbert a success in business. Meanwhile the Newgate and Satis House strands continue to parallel this inner struggle. Pip's sense of guilt, the vagueness and intensity of which make it seem almost like original sin, is symbolized by the Newgate motif of crime and punishment; his pride and ambition are reflected in the Estella–Miss Havisham configuration of jeweled elegance grounded in decay and hurt vanity. In one scene Pip is at Satis House, priding himself on his expectations; in another he is in front of Newgate prison, feeling inexplicable guilt.

In this section Dickens begins to draw the two strands together, in order to prepare for the revelation of Magwitch as Pip's benefactor at the end of Part Two. In a regular pattern, the Magwitch strand presses more and more into the foreground (every fourth chapter now instead of every fifth), working toward its emergence into the surface of the novel. In Chapter XX Pip first feels the oppressive horror of Newgate; in Chapter XXIV he watches Jaggers at work in court, among felons and convicts; in Chapter XXVIII he meets the convict with the aiming eye again; in Chapter XXXII, after touring Newgate, he feels himself contaminated by the convicts and their crimes, and recalling earlier experiences of the same sort, he begins intuitively to connect Estella with his guilt; in Chapter XXXVI he comes of age and recklessly presses Jaggers for information about his benefactor; finally, in Chapter XXXIX, when Magwitch reveals himself as Pip's benefactor, the hidden strand emerges and the illusion of the apparent strand crumbles away:

> All the work, near and afar, that tended to the end, had been accomplished; and in an instant the blow was struck, and the roof of my stronghold dropped upon me.

This is the discovery and reversal. . . .

The emerging hidden strand of events and the apparent strand it displaces are reflections of Pip's inner self, and with discovery and reversal in the plot also begins a similar violent turning about within the character of the hero. But this "character recognition" comes slowly and painfully, for the very reason that it involves giving up so much. Not only Pip, but Dickens himself holds back from the true meaning of the dream, because it contains his own fears and desires as well as his hero's. Still, simply because it contains them, the meaning must be worked out; something must be imagined to bring them to a temporary resolution. After the explosive scene of discovery, the pieces of Pip's world must be picked up and put back together in a new configuration. When the hidden strand emerges in the discovery, it becomes the dominant sequence of action in the dream structure, and takes over the surface of the narrative from the apparent strand it has "reversed." However, some threads of the displaced pattern, although they no longer function as they once did, remain to be accounted for and woven into the new structure of meaning. The gathering up of these broken threads constitutes the resolution, and the end comes when the possibilities of integration have been used up.

The method by which Dickens weaves the frayed ends of the Satis House strand into the fabric of the whole consists of a series of what must be called "secondary discoveries"— of secret family relationships, hidden motives, the buried past. These secondary discoveries are not merely melodramatic devices to wind up the story somehow, nor are they simply adjuncts to the primary discovery; because they represent Pip's world, the avoided and delayed recognition of the truth of his own feelings and actions, they have their own special function in freeing the hero to act out his destiny.

Food in *Great Expectations*

Barbara Hardy

Barbara Hardy, professor emeritus of literature at the University of London, compares meals in *Great Expectations*. In one kind of meal, food is provided and eaten only to fulfill a biological need, with no moral significance. But when love and thankfulness are given and received along with the food in another kind of meal, it is a beacon of moral meaning in the world of the novel, which is otherwise fairly dark. Ironically, it is the meal that the young Pip steals and that Magwitch wolfs down in the marshes that is characterized by affection and gratitude, as Hardy clearly demonstrates, and this meal has a moral significance that reverberates throughout the novel. In contrast, the meals that Pip is served by Estella and Mrs. Joe are merely biological at best. Perhaps most strikingly, so is the meal the grown-up Pip gives Magwitch in London, after Pip has risen in society. Barbara Hardy has also written critical studies of nineteenth-century British novelists Jane Austen, William Makepeace Thackeray, and George Eliot.

The first meal in *Great Expectations* is *demanded* in the first chapter. Magwitch in desperate hunger terrifies Pip into stealing food: 'You know what wittles is . . . you get me wittles.' In the third chapter Pip brings the food, and Magwitch makes the first response of gratitude which begins the long chain of obligation, illusion, pride, and love. It is necessary to see what moves his gratitude: it is not the mere provision of food, important though this is. Pip is doing more than satisfy the physical need, he is allowing nature more than nature needs. Magwitch is eating like a beast but Pip treats him as a guest and makes him respond as a guest:

Excerpted from *The Moral Art of Dickens*, by Barbara Hardy. Copyright 1970 by Barbara Hardy. Reprinted with permission from The Athlone Press Ltd.

He was already handing mincemeat down his throat in the most curious manner—more like a man who was putting it away somewhere in a violent hurry, than a man who was eating it—but he left off to take some of the liquor. He shivered all the while so violently, that it was quite as much as he could do to keep the neck of the bottle between his teeth, without biting it off. . . .

He was gobbling mincemeat, meat bone, bread, cheese, and pork pie, all at once: staring distrustfully while he did so at the mist all round us, and often stopping—even stopping his jaws—to listen.

This is a grotesque table, spread in the wilderness of mist and marshes for a man who is wolfing down the food out of fear. Pip is no more in the conventional position of host than Magwitch is in the conventional position of guest, but the very lack of ceremony moves Pip to do more than steal and give in terror and in minimal satisfaction of need. Pity moves him to sauce the meat with ceremony and turn it into something more. . . . Pip's ceremony has special point in this bare rough meeting where the guest is desperate and the host terrorized:

Pitying his desolation . . . I made bold to say, 'I am glad you enjoy it.'

'Did you speak?'

'I said, I am glad you enjoyed it.'

'Thankee, my boy. I do.'

The child's civility and pity take no offence from his guest's table-manners. These are carefully observed, without revulsion:

I had often watched a large dog of ours eating his food; and now I noticed a decided similarity between the dog's way of eating, and the man's. The man took strong sharp sudden bites, just like the dog. He swallowed, or rather snapped up, every mouthful, too soon and too fast; and he looked sideways here and there while he ate, as if he thought there was danger in every direction of somebody's coming to take the pie away. He was altogether too unsettled in his mind over it, to appreciate it comfortably, I thought, or to have anybody to dine with him, without making a chop with his jaws at the visitor. In all of which particulars he was very like the dog.

The detached account makes the politeness more marked. It is apparent that Pip's naïve comparisons, to the dog and to more comfortable meals, imply no sense of social superiority, though the social implications are plain to the reader. Pip is not repelled by the resemblance to the dog, but is sorry for it, and instead of treating the man like a dog, gives with love. The 'I am glad you enjoy it' and the 'Thankee' turn the rudest meal in the novel into an introductory model of ceremony. What makes the ceremony is love, generosity, and gratitude. I need not labour the attachment of this scene to the main themes of the novel.

This meal acts as a model of ceremony, and controls our response to the many related descriptions of meals which succeed it. The gratitude and compassionate love are both present in chapter V, when Magwitch lies about stealing the food, to protect Pip, and is answered by Joe: 'God knows you're welcome to it—so far as it was ever mine. . . . We don't know what you have done, but we wouldn't have you starved to death for it, poor miserable fellow-creatur.—Would us, Pip?'. . .

An Unsatisfying Meal

The beginning of his illusory great expectations, like the beginning of the real ones, is marked by a significant meal. Estella is the hostess, Pip the guest. The meal is less grotesque than the meal with Magwitch but it too lacks the ceremonious cover of a roof, for Estella tells Pip to wait in the yard:

> She came back, with some bread and meat and a little mug of beer. She put the mug down on the stones of the yard, and gave me the bread and meat without looking at me, as insolently as if I were a dog in disgrace. I was so humiliated, hurt, spurned, offended, angry, sorry—I cannot hit upon the right name for the smart—God knows what its name was—that tears started to my eyes.

The contrast is clinched by the comparison with the dog. Pip's full wants are not satisfied, even though this is the hospitality of Satis House, but in terms of physical need he is given enough. He is treated like a dog, given no more than nature needs, but he does not lose his appetite any more than Magwitch, treated with courtesy, stops eating like a dog. Dickens makes this distinction unsentimentally and truthfully, merely allowing Pip to observe that 'the bread and food were acceptable, and the beer was warming and tingling, and I was soon in spirits to look about me'. Like Magwitch, and for similar reasons of protective love, Pip lies about this meal. His sense of humiliation and his desire to protect Estella from 'the contemplation of Mrs Joe' makes him elaborate the marvellous childish fantasy about the 'cake and wine on gold plates', which Pumblechook and Joe and Mrs Joe, in their social innocence, accept. Pip invents a meal appropriate to Satis House, and hides his shame, but he preserves both the hierarchy and the bizarre quality of his encounter by placing the meal in a coach, and saying that he 'got up behind the coach to eat mine, because she told me to'. Even the dog comes back, magnified into 'four immense dogs' who come off rather better than Pip did since they fight 'for veal-cutlets out of a silver basket'. On his next visit to Satis House we return briefly to the dog: 'I was taken into the yard to be fed in the former dog-like manner.' The two meals respond in perfect antithesis.

DOGLIKE EATING, UNDOGLIKE COURTESY

The first ceremony of love finds another responsive scene when Magwitch discloses his responsibility and motivation to Pip. We are carefully reminded of the first meal on the marshes: 'I drops my knife many a time in that hut when I was a eating my dinner or my supper, and I says, "Here's the boy again, a looking at me whiles I eats and drinks!"'

It is to this actual memory of the meal that he attaches his plan to 'make that boy a gentleman' but when the gentleman serves him with a meal he does not look at him as the boy did:

> He ate in a ravenous manner that was very disagreeable, and all his actions were uncouth, noisy, and greedy. Some of his teeth had failed him since I saw him eat on the marshes, and as he turned his food in his mouth, and turned his head sideways to bring his strongest fangs to bear upon it, he looked terribly like a hungry old dog.

> If I had begun with any appetite, he would have taken it away, and I should have sat much as I did—repelled from him by an insurmountable aversion, and gloomily looking at the cloth.

The uncouth eating, the hunger, the sideways movement, and the comparison with the dog are repetitions from the early scene which emphasize the distance between the child and the man. This time the observation is full of revulsion, the food is not sauced with ceremony. But if the host has changed, the guest has not, and he apologizes for his doglike eating with undoglike courtesy:

> 'I'm a heavy grubber, dear boy,' he said, as a polite kind of apology when he had made an end of his meal, 'but I always was. If it had been in my constitution to be a lighter grubber, I might ha' got into lighter trouble.'

The apology is made without shame or self-pity on the part of Magwitch, and provokes no sympathy on the part of

Pip. In the early scene the child's pity was impulsive and provoked simply by the desperate eating and panic. In the later scenes, Pip is in a position to see the connection between the heavy grubbing and the heavy trouble, but describes without pity the roughness and greed: 'there was Prisoner, Felon, Bondsman, plain as plain could be'. . . .

EATING ON PINS AND NEEDLES

Magwitch tells Pip and Herbert how his heavy grubbing explains his troubled career and begins his life-story with the little boy who stole turnips and who was always driven by the need 'to put something into his stomach'. Pip as a child is not physically deprived in this way, but although he is given enough to eat, he is not given his food with love. In Chapter ii, between Magwitch's demand for food and Pip's generous response, we are given a glimpse of Mrs Joe's 'bringing up by hand'. She is an unloving mother-surrogate who feeds her family unceremoniously:

> My sister had a trenchant way of cutting our bread-and-butter for us, that never varied. First, with her left hand she jammed the loaf hard and fast against her bib—where it sometimes got a pin into it, and sometimes a needle, which we afterwards got into our mouths. Then she took some butter (not too much) on a knife and spread it on the loaf, in an apothecary kind of way, as if she were making a plaister—using both sides of the knife with a slapping dexterity, and trimming and moulding the butter off round the crust. Then, she gave the knife a final smart wipe on the edge of the plaister.

The pins and needles have already been mentioned as characteristic of this unmotherly breast: 'She was tall and bony, and almost always wore a coarse apron, fastened over her figure behind with two loops, and having a square impregnable bib in front, that was stuck full of pins and needles.'

Some of the implications of this juxtaposition are terrifying, but the Gargery household is treated with comedy rather than with harsh violence. . . . The moral implications within the novel are plain: Mrs Joe gives unlovingly, to put it mildly, taking most pleasure in the administration of Tar-Water and fasts, while Joe shares the wedges of bread in love and play, and tries to make up for Pip's sufferings at the Christmas dinner with spoonfulls of gravy. . . .

Food in *Great Expectations* is part of the public order, and the meals testify to human need and dependence, and distinguish false ceremony from the ceremony of love.

Examining the Role of Magwitch

Robin Gilmour

Pip's great expectations of rising in society and marrying Estella come crashing down when he learns that his benefactor is not the aristocratic Miss Havisham but the criminal Abel Magwitch. University of Aberdeen English professor Robin Gilmour focuses on Magwitch as, first of all, a representative of all the suffering and violence Pip is trying to escape by rising in society. When it is revealed that Magwitch is Estella's father as well as Pip's benefactor, it is clear that upper-class life is as full of crime and cruelty as the lower-class life at the forge and on the marshes. Magwitch, Gilmour argues, is thus the agent of Pip's disillusionment and the truth of his underlying reality and his dreams. Ironically, Magwitch has been the source of both Pip's rise in society and his fall from it; and in the final third of the novel, he becomes the source of Pip's rise as a man when Pip learns to recognize him not as a criminal to be ashamed of, but as a human being to love.

[Pip's] predicament is representative of a social class in the act of emergence; specifically, of the Victorian middle class in its emergence from primitive origins. He *needs* civilisation because he is so acutely aware (as the born gentleman Herbert cannot be) of its opposite, and consequently he overvalues it, purging his advance into gentility from all associations with the physical brutality which had formed his 'first most vivid and broad impression of the identity of things'. Satis House comes to symbolise 'everything that was picturesque', and it captures Pip's imagination just because it seems to be the negation of all that he has known on the marshes. Estella is so utterly divorced in his mind from any association with criminality that (in one of the many brilliantly economical symbolic touches in which the novel abounds) he cannot bear Jaggers even to sit next to her at the card-table, trumping 'the glory of our Kings and Queens . . . with mean little cards at the ends of hands'. While waiting for her at the coach-house near Newgate he feels contaminated by his recent visit to the jail with Wemmick:

> I thought of the beautiful young Estella, proud and refined, coming towards me, and I thought with absolute abhorrence of the contrast between the jail and her. I wished that Wemmick had not met me, or that I had not yielded to him and gone with him, so that, of all days in the year on this day, I might not have had Newgate in my breath and on my clothes.

Yet the very intensity with which Pip repudiates this contrast betrays a nagging consciousness of interrelationship between the areas of his experience which he wants to keep apart. He is, one might say, the conscience of his environment, for he has to carry within himself a secret knowledge of the polarities which make up his world. The blacksmith's boy who aspires to being a gentleman can never know the certainty of status which Herbert inherits as a matter of course; at home in neither world, he experiences a continual remorse and a moral isolation which align him, paradoxically, with the criminal outcast who constitutes his most enduring image of all that the civilised life will free him from. Pip's sense of guilt, I would suggest, is the subconscious recognition of a truth which he deeply resents, in common with the Victorian middle-class culture of which he may be said to be a pioneer: that criminality and civilisation, violence and refinement, Magwitch and Estella, are not warring opposites but intimately and inextricably bound together.

The basic *donnée* of the book, the pivot on which Dickens's 'grotesque tragi-comic conception' turns, is the fact that Magwitch is Pip's benefactor and the father of Estella. But so firm is Dickens's control of his theme, so subtle his command of significant detail, that long before the convict's return he has been able to suggest this inherent contradiction in his hero's expectations. The narrative is indeed a fabric of wonderful richness and resonance. For example, when Pip visits Satis House for the second time the smoke from the dining-room fire reminds him of 'our own marsh mist' , just as the cobwebs on Miss Havisham's bridal cake recall the damp on the hedges, like 'a coarser sort of spiders' webs', on the morning when he sneaks out of the forge to carry the food to Magwitch. Such delicate tracery of interrelationship serves to unify the atmosphere of the novel, undermining the opposition Pip is setting up between the savagery of the marshes and the refinement of Satis House, and thereby preparing the way for the revelations to come.

The separation of the two worlds is also undermined in the case of Bentley Drummle, Pip's rival for Estella, a minor character who foreshadows an important truth which is only fully manifest at the end of *Great Expectations.* As his name implies, with its suggestion of 'bend', 'drum', and 'pummel', Drummle is heavy, brutish, cruel and violent; he is an upper-class equivalent of the journeyman Orlick, with whom he is associated at the end of chapter 43. The function of this character in the scheme of the novel is to remind us that violence and brutality are not confined to life on the marshes, that they also exist in the supposedly refined society of London. And Estella's marriage to Drummle provides another dimension to our understanding of her character. This 'proud and refined' girl who is the very incarnation of the civilised life to which Pip aspires can prefer a coarse brute like Drummle because there exists, deep within her, a violent animal nature which Pip ignores. Dickens suggests this fact in chapter 11, where Pip fights and beats Herbert. Unknown to him, Estella has been watching the fight and when she comes down to let him out 'there was a bright flush upon her face, as though something had happened to delight her'. She offers to let Pip kiss her, and he does so, without realising the significance of her sudden response; he feels that 'the kiss was given to the coarse common boy as a piece of money might have been, and that it was worth nothing'. The brief scene enacts the supreme paradox of Pip's life: Estella can only respond to him when he exhibits those qualities of physical force and animal aggression which, in order to win her, he is at pains to civilise out of himself. It is her one spontaneous gesture to Pip and he misreads it, feeling only guilt and remorse at this exercise of his blacksmith's arm. . . .

PIP'S ESCAPE FAILS

It is Pip's self-conscious revulsion from the violence of life on the marshes which sets him apart from his home and decides him to become a gentleman, and it is this violence, in the shape of Magwitch, which provides the ultimate touch-stone for the values and social position he has embraced. The most intimate meaning of Dickens's fable of social evolution is finally revealed when the old convict returns, and brings with him not only the truth about the source of Pip's wealth, but also a fearful reassertion of the primitive forces from which he had thought to have escaped forever:

> The influences of his solitary hut-life were upon him besides, and gave him a savage air that no dress could tame; added to these were the influences of his subsequent branded life among men, and crowning all, his consciousness that he was dodging and hiding now. In all his ways of sitting and standing, and eating and drinking—of brooding about, in a high-shouldered reluctant style—of taking out his great horn-handled jack-knife and wiping it on his legs and cutting his food—of lifting light glasses and cups to his lips, as if they were clumsy pannikins—of chopping a wedge off his bread, and soaking up with it the last fragments of gravy round and

THE SHOE POLISH WAREHOUSE AND DICKENS'S NEED TO ESCAPE

A shameful experience of social humiliation in Dickens's own childhood made him desperate to escape into respectability, just as Pip is ashamed of his blacksmith's hands when he aspires to rise to Estella's level in society. At twelve years old, Dickens was sent to work twelve hours a day in Warren's Blacking, a shoe polish warehouse on the dirty, crumbling London waterfront. He gave this account of his experience there to his close friend John Forster.

The deep remembrance of the sense I had of being utterly neglected and hopeless; of the shame I felt in my position; of the misery it was to my young heart to believe that, day by day, what I had learned, and thought, and delighted in, and raised my fancy and my emulation up by, was passing away from me, never to be brought back any more; cannot be written. . . .

Bob (who was much bigger and older than I) did not like the idea of my going home alone, and took me under his protection. I was too proud to let him know about the prison; and after making several efforts to get rid of him, to all of which Bob Fagin in his goodness was deaf, shook hands with him on the steps of a house near Southwark Bridge on the Surrey side, making believe that I lived there.

John Forster, *The Life of Charles Dickens*, 2 vols. London: J.M. Dent & Sons, 1966 reprint, vol. I, pp. 21–33.

round his plate, as if to make the most of an allowance, and then drying his fingers on it, and then swallowing it . . . there was Prisoner, Felon, Bondsman, plain as plain could be . . .

Words cannot tell what a sense I had, at the same time, of the dreadful mystery that he was to me. When he fell asleep of an evening, with his knotted hands clenching the sides of the easy-chair, and his bald head tattooed with deep wrinkles falling forward on his breast, I would sit and look at him, wondering what he had done, and loading him with all the crimes in the Calendar, until the impulse was powerful on me to start up and fly from him.

Magwitch is the embodiment of everything Pip has tried to free himself from, even down to the 'heavy grubbing' which is only an exaggerated form of the clumsy table-manners Pip had acquired at the forge. He is also a violent criminal, and for all Pip knows a man with blood on his hands; he recalls with horror his childhood vision of the convict as a 'desperately violent man' whom he had seen 'down in the ditch, tearing and fighting like a wild beast'. Yet such is the symbolic suggestiveness of Dickens's conception, that this wild beast, a returned transport, is in his way a nightmare version of the Victorian self-made man. (Even here one can see something of Dickens's literal and imaginative fidelity to the period setting of his novel. It was a fact that in the early years of the colonisation of Australia many emancipated convicts did make huge fortunes. Giving evidence before the 1837 Select Committee on Transportation, John Lang, a Church of Scotland clergyman in New South Wales, cited the case of one convict who was reputed to have an annual income of £40,000, and agreed that there were many who had 'some thousands a year'. They made their fortunes 'generally very rapidly', Lang said, because they 'bent the whole energy of mind and body to money making'.) Magwitch has pursued wealth with a single-mindedness which makes his career in Australia a bizarre parody of the classic economic success story: 'I lived rough', he tells Pip, echoing the paternal hopes of first-generation wealth, 'that you should live smooth; I worked hard that you should be above work'.

What is the significance of Magwitch in the novel? He is the father of Estella, the 'proud and refined' girl who is the very emblem and model of the civilised life to which Pip aspires; and theirs is a blood-relationship in a double sense, for we have already seen that Estella possesses an animal will and energy and passion, a deeply-seated physical nature which Pip ignores in his idealisation of her. The moral pattern of *Great Expectations* is only fulfilled when, in chapter 48, Jaggers hints that Bentley Drummle will beat Estella, and Pip, glancing at Molly's knitting fingers and flowing hair, realises that this woman is the mother of the girl he loves. The wheel has come full circle; the girl who had been the inspiration for his attempt to improve himself is found in the end to be the daughter of a transported convict and 'a wild beast tamed', a woman so violent and powerful that she has been able to strangle another woman with her bare hands. And what in a lesser novelist would be a melodramatic linkage is here a symbolic structure of deep imaginative power and social implication. This triangular relationship of 'blood' ramifies throughout the novel, destroying the opposition Pip has set up between the worlds of the marshes, Satis House and London.

Magwitch is the ultimate source of all Pip's expectations. With his energy, his resourcefulness, his powerful will and rough sense of justice, his touching respect for the refinements of life expressed in admiration for his 'dear boy's' dubious accomplishments, he is a grotesque parody of the uncouth but successful self-made man, determined that his son shall be a gentleman. In recoiling from him, Pip, like the fastidious Victorian gentleman he has by that stage become, is understandably recoiling from contemplating the unpleasant social origins of the wealth that makes gentlemanliness possible—from facing the fact that the economic security which has enabled him to work out the beast was itself provided by bestial means. What Pip has to experience in the concluding third of the novel is the unweaving of the spell that has bound him hitherto; he has to learn that Magwitch is not an ogre but a human being, and a decent and generous one; that Estella, 'proud and refined', has the same blood flowing through her veins; and that the opposition he has set up between the two worlds is false. And in learning the truth about the ultimate interrelatedness of a society based upon class distinctions, he learns to overcome the division within himself, between the inhibited, guilt-ridden gentleman he has become and the blacksmith's boy he has locked away and failed to acknowledge in his pursuit of gentility. . . .

THE HOLDING OF HANDS

With the unveiling of illusion Pip overcomes his revulsion from Magwitch; the blacksmith's boy and the gentleman are integrated in the physical gesture of holding the old convict's hand in the boat and later, publicly, at his trial: 'For now, my repugnance to him had all melted away, and in the hunted wounded shackled creature who held my hand in his, I only saw a man who had meant to be my benefactor, and who had felt affectionately, gratefully, and generously, towards me with great constancy through a series of years. I only saw in him a much better man than I had been to Joe'. And it is appropriate that in the illness which follows Magwitch's death Pip should be nursed back to health by Joe in an episode which returns him, briefly and poignantly, to the old physical intimacy and dependence of childhood. Pip cannot be a child again, or preserve the old companionship once he has recovered; but Joe can heal him out of the 'wealth of his great nature', his physical tenderness can penetrate the crust of genteel inhibition and release the flow of feeling which has for so long been trapped beneath. Again, this release and reintegration is signalled in the holding of hands:

At last, one day, I took courage, and said, '*Is* it Joe?'

And the dear old home-voice answered, 'Which it air, old chap.'

'O Joe, you break my heart! Look angry at me, Joe. Strike me, Joe. Tell me of my ingratitude. Don't be so good to me!'

For Joe had actually laid his head down on the pillow at my side, and put his arm round my neck, in his joy that I knew him.

'Which dear old Pip, old chap,' said Joe, 'you and me was ever friends. And when you're well enough to go out for a ride— what larks!'

After which, Joe withdrew to the window, and stood with his back towards me, wiping his eyes. And as my extreme weakness prevented me from getting up and going to him, I lay there, penitently whispering, 'O God bless him! O God bless this gentle Christian man!'

Joe's eyes were red when I next found him beside me; but I was holding his hand and we both felt happy.

'O God bless this gentle Christian man!' Pip (and Dickens) separate the word 'gentleman' into its classless elements, the gentle man who, living by the Christian ideals of love and forgiveness, is the one type of gentlemanliness which the novel at the end unequivocally affirms.

Fearful Dreams

Claire Slagter

Pip frequently describes his dreams in *Great Expectations*, and these episodes reveal his inner psychological turmoil in the course of the narrative. Dickens scholar and critic Claire Slagter traces the pattern of anxiety, fright, guilt, and self-contempt portrayed in Pip's dreams. In addition, she notes that Dickens places these dreams at key turning points in the story: 1) right after Pip meets Magwitch, 2) right after he meets Miss Havisham, 3) right before he leaves for London, 4) shortly before he begins to recognize his own egotism, and 5) right after he has been confronted by Magwitch and recognizes their bond. Once Pip has fully embraced Magwitch and renounced his own social pretensions, his agitation diminishes and his self-esteem improves. And when Pip finally accepts himself for what he is, the heavy burden of living a shallow, phony life is lightened. At that point, he ceases to dream.

Pip's expectations begin with his encounter with Magwitch and his dreaming begins there too:

> If I slept at all that night, it was only to imagine myself drifting down the river on a strong spring-tide, to the Hulks; a ghostly pirate calling out to me through a speaking-trumpet, as I passed the gibbet-station, that I had better come ashore and be hanged there at once, and not put it off.

Fear, guilt and the certainty of retribution are already revealed in this dream as the distinctive characteristics of Pip's personality marked, as the mature Pip notes when considering his childhood, by a kind of 'cowardice' and 'moral timidity'. And these are the traits which are repeatedly suggested by the numerous other dreams which Pip records in his narrative.

In Chapter 10 Pip is in the village inn with Joe when he sees a stranger who stirs his rum-and-water with a file. Pip recognizes the file as the one he stole from Joe to help the convict. He is then given:

Reprinted from "Pip's Dreams in *Great Expectations*," by Claire Slagter, *The Dickensian*, vol. 83, no. 413, Autumn 1987, pp. 180–83.

> Nothing less than two fat sweltering one-pound notes . . . My
> sister . . . put them . . . in an ornamental teapot on the top of
> a press in the state parlour. There they remained, a night-
> mare to me, many and many a night and day.
>
> I had sadly broken sleep when I got to bed, through thinking
> of the strange man taking aim at me with his invisible gun,
> and of the guiltily coarse and common thing it was, to be on
> secret terms of conspiracy with convicts—a feature in my low
> career that I had previously forgotten. I was haunted by the
> file too. A dread possessed me that when I least expected it,
> the file would reappear. I coaxed myself to sleep by thinking
> of Miss Havisham's, next Wednesday; and in my sleep I saw
> the file coming at me out of a door, without seeing who held
> it, and screamed myself awake.

On a psychological level this summarises the power of
Pip's guilt and low self-esteem. It is a common dream
process to relive the experiences of the day as preoccupa-
tions recur to us in dreams. Pip's guilty feelings overcome
him. On a structural level this dream puts an end to the
chapter and determines the mode of our reaction to this part
of Pip's life. It is an interesting fact that Charles Dickens put
this passage right at the end of a chapter and at the end of an
instalment as well. The dreams or nightmares that are
placed at the end of a chapter indicate that Dickens planned
them as a point of reflection for the reader, reflection concerning not only the facts, but more important still, a re-
assessment of our attitudes to those events. Significantly,
Dickens mentions the image Pip invokes to coax himself to
sleep, Miss Havisham. Their dreams coincide. Pip is not only
part of Miss Havisham's 'dream' of revenge, she is also part
of his daydream, his illusion that she intends him to marry
Estella.

LEAVING BEHIND A CHILDHOOD NIGHTMARE

Pip's next dream has to do with this illusion as well. It occurs
again towards the end of a chapter and the end of an instalment and it sets the tone for the end of this part of Pip's expectations. He has had his fortune announced to him and he
prepares to go to London to enter upon a new life there. He
wishes to leave the nightmarish atmosphere of his childhood guilt behind him, without realizing that he will only
enter into the daydream, the wishful thinking of the convict
Magwitch. The last night he spends in his childhood home
is described at the end of Chapter 19:

All night there were coaches in my broken sleep, going to wrong places instead of to London, and having in the traces, now dogs, now cats, now pigs, now men—never horses. Fantastic failures of journeys occupied me until the day dawned and the birds were singing. Then, I got up and partly dressed, and sat at the window to take a last look out, and in taking it fell asleep.

This dream is not only put towards the end of the chapter but also towards the end of: '. . . THE FIRST STAGE OF PIP'S EXPECTATIONS'. Once more it has the function of giving the reader a glimpse of Pip's inner life. This dream gives insight into the character Pip develops in the second stage of his expectations. Pip turns into a snob who feels above the people he used to be familiar with, Joe, his sister and Biddy who has taken her place in the household. Pip plans to go to London in order to become a man of the world. It is natural that he should be full of dreams then, both at night and in the daytime. But in the daytime he refuses Joe's company when Joe offers to walk him to the coach, and at night he is visited by his guilty conscience and knows very well that his attitude is slightly ridiculous. Again, it is a visual dream where different animals draw the coach which takes Pip to London, 'Never horses' Pip says. And anyway the coach does not even go to London, as Pip says 'Fantastic failures . . .' where the alliteration draws extra attention to Pip's worried night thoughts. The coach is drawn by dogs—not so surprising and not all that ridiculous—by cats—slightly more odd if visualized but still domestic animals which convey some notion of civilization to the reader. But the next example in this list puts a stop to that, for it is pigs that are in the traces now, that otherwise roll in the mud and the dung. Whatever could be expected as the next step in this vision, it is certainly not men. Yet this is what Pip sees in his dream. Apparently, he ranks his fellow human beings lower than dogs, cats, even pigs. The whole night Pip goes from one extreme to another—when he dreams of being in a coach drawn by men he feels miles above other people—but then he wakes up time and again—'broken sleep' only to go back to more dreams in the same vein. His unconscious thoughts have sent a mutilated message to his conscious by means of the dream. This dream is not only an example of Dickens's humour for it goes deeper than that. In the dream Pip is shown as the snob he is turning into, setting out to London where he will spend his fortune rather than make it. The dream can therefore be taken as an indicator of this change in development of the novel and determines the response of the reader to a great extent.

DISTURBING DAYS, FITFUL DREAMS

That the next example of a dream should occur towards the end of a chapter and at the end of an instalment—Chapter 31, the final paragraph—is in keeping with what we have seen so far:

> Miserably I went to bed after all, and miserably thought of Estella, and miserably dreamed that my expectations were all cancelled, and that I had to give my hand in marriage to Herbert's Clara, or play Hamlet to Miss Havisham's Ghost, before twenty thousand people, without knowing twenty words of it.

Pip and Herbert have dined with Mr Wopsle—an entertainment that leaves Pip miserable as we are told three times in the above passage. It is with these feelings that the reader enters the next chapter—miserable thoughts of Estella, of expectations that are all cancelled, or marriage to the wrong woman, however right she may be for Herbert,—the chapter in which Pip gets a note from Estella arranging to meet her at the coach office, a meeting that raises Pip's hopes high again. This is a good example of a dream which sums up the proceedings of the chapter. At the same time it is a dream that provides a link with the next chapter where Pip is in higher spirits. The symbols of this dream are very important, not only in their own right but also because they determine the reactions of the reader. The dreams clearly seem to be intended to guide the reader's emotions as we respond to Pip's disorientation and instability.

On a psychological level it is interesting to notice that Pip has his miserable dream immediately after meeting with Mr Wopsle—the pompous, flaunting, man. It is suggested in modern psychology that if we dislike a person it is our own bad characteristics we recognize and deplore in him. Charles Dickens may intuitively have felt this and inserted this clue to show the reader that Pip is about to arrive at a turning point in his self obsessed career.

AN OUTLET FOR FEAR

An instance of a dream made light of and yet retaining its significance comes at the end of Chapter 40 when Magwitch, now called Provis, has just come to London where he proudly visits Pip, his protégé, to whom he is a constant 'nightmare':

> Expecting Herbert all the time, I dared not go out, except
> when I took Provis for an airing after dark. At length, one
> evening when dinner was over and I had dropped into a
> slumber quite worn out—for my nights had been agitated and
> my rest was broken by fearful dreams—I was roused by the
> welcome footsteps on the staircase.

The 'fearful dreams' mentioned here create the mood in
which the reader shares Pip's experience of Provis's arrival
and stay, but they also give more information. They prove
that Pip's everyday life—constantly looking after Provis who
has become Pip's dangerous ward rather than benefactor—
is getting too much for him. On a psychological level it is
natural that disturbing days should find an outlet in one's
dreams at night and on a structural level it is natural as well
for the writer to mention the fact that the main character is
occupied—day and night—with a matter so important in his
life. If previous dreams signalled turning points this one can
certainly claim to be one. After all it is here that Pip reviews
his past life and errors. He understands how mistaken he
has been and he resolves to change his way of life. It is also
a turning point in that the dreams and the daydreams
change, Pip is part of Magwitch's 'daydream' of making a
gentleman until he becomes Pip's nightmare.

PREMONITIONS

After this it is Pip who tries to control events and who
dreams again:

> With this project formed, we went to bed. I had the wildest
> dreams concerning him, and woke unrefreshed; I woke, too, to
> recover the fear which I had lost in the night, of his being found
> out as a returned transport. Waking, I never lost that fear.

If previously the dreams were taken as the warnings of a
troubled conscience or guilty feelings that were pushed
away in the daytime only to return at night, this time it
seems that they are dreams concerning things to come, as is
obvious from another passage in the same chapter when Pip
talks to Herbert about what action to take now: 'I have seen
it, Herbert, and dreamed of it, ever since that fatal night of
his arrival. Nothing has been in my thoughts so distinctly as
his putting himself in the way of being taken'.

The keyword is 'fear' and fear pervades these passages as
it pervades Pip's whole life. This time it is fear of being found
out, not fear of what he has done before. Still, as a structural
device it serves the same purpose, it draws extra attention to

what happens at the level of the plot and it serves as the turning point, a moment when the emotions are running highest and undergo major changes. Once Pip realises that the second stage of his great expectations is over, he changes into a mature young man, having come to terms with reality and poverty, no longer part of someone else's dream.

CHAPTER 3

The Character of Pip

Pip's Personal Journey to Adulthood

Paul Pickrel

Paul Pickrel, for many years editor of the *Yale Review*, outlines the theme of Pip's personal growth in terms of his graduation from a childish world of fantasy into an adult world of moral responsibility. Experience teaches Pip that the childhood world is full of illusions: Miss Havisham is not a fairy godmother after all, Estella is not a princess, and Magwitch is not a monster. To grow, Pip must leave these childish fantasies behind and enter the real world of adult choices with moral consequences. Pip is morally educated by Joe's warm heart and Mr. Jaggers's clear eye, but as Pickrel points out, the moral transition from childhood to adulthood is not an easy one for Pip.

The story is a fairy tale, with a terrible ogre, Magwitch, a wildly eccentric fairy godmother, an exquisite princess, and a sudden magical transformation. But it is not only a fairy tale, for it is set in a moral universe. One beauty of the life of fantasy, and one reason some of us devote so much time to it, is that it is free from considerations of good and evil. In fantasy we kill off our friends and relatives with impunity; we grow rich without effort; we bestow lavish presents without impoverishing ourselves; we live in immense houses without concern for the servant problem. The moral universe is quite different from that: there our acts have consequences, our choices matter, our privileges entail responsibilities.

Now, just as Dickens defines the world of fantasy by two characters, or groups of characters, Magwitch on the one hand, and Miss Havisham and Estella on the other, so he defines the moral universe by two groups of characters, one group centered on Pip's brother-in-law, the blacksmith Joe Gargery, and the other centered on the London lawyer, Mr. Jaggers, who brings Pip word of his great expectations. Or perhaps that is not quite accurate: Dickens uses Joe and Mr. Jaggers not to define the moral universe—that is done by the plot—but rather to personify or embody two different attitudes toward it.

THE HEART VS. THE HEAD

Joe lives by truth to feeling and Mr. Jaggers lives by truth to fact. Joe characteristically looks at a situation as a whole and relates himself to it as his heart bids him. Mr. Jaggers characteristically breaks the situation down into "evidence" and disposes of the evidence in whatever way his mind tells him is appropriate. Joe holds a poetic or symbolic view of experience; Mr. Jaggers holds an analytical. If Joe, for example, had come across Christina Rossetti's line, "My heart is like a singing bird," he would have known just what she meant, because he would have recognized its truth to feeling; but if Mr. Jaggers had come across the line he would have asked with a snort, "Tell me, Miss Rossetti, precisely what color are the feathers on your heart?" because the evidence that the chief organ of the circulatory system in fact resembles a singing fowl is extremely meagre.

At the bottom the difference between the two men lies in a difference in their sense of how things are related in the universe and, consequently, in their sense of how an individual can relate himself to them. This comes out most strikingly when we look at the way the two men have behaved in roughly parallel situations. Before the novel opens each man has come across a mother and baby, and each man has responded to the situation in a highly characteristic manner. Joe Gargery came across Pip and his older sister, who was attempting to bring the baby up singlehanded. Joe wanted to help the child, and he did so by embracing the situation as a whole. Though the sister was a termagant with little in her nature to bring the idea of matrimony to a man's mind, Joe married her and so became a kind of father to the baby. Mr. Jaggers, on the other hand, came across a young woman with a baby girl, and his method of dealing with the situation was to separate them. The child he put out for adoption where she would never know who her mother was, and the mother he took into his own house, not on terms of affection but as a servant kept in place by terror. The situations are not strictly parallel, because the future Mrs. Joe Gargery was only a shrew, whereas Mr. Jaggers' future servant was actually a criminal and her baby daughter the child of another criminal, but there is enough similarity to indicate the moral points of view of the two men.

Another way that the difference is dramatized is in the way the two men relate themselves to Pip. Joe's relationship is based upon feeling for the boy, and he allows nothing to cloud the purity of that feeling. This is brilliantly dramatized in the scene where Miss Havisham insists on paying Pip's premium as an apprentice. Joe had never expected such a premium, of course; he expected to take Pip as an apprentice because he loved him. So when Miss Havisham summons them to Satis House, Joe addresses all his remarks to Pip; the money he cannot decline, but he flatly refuses to turn a relationship based on love into a commercial transaction. In speaking to Miss Havisham only through Pip he asserts that nothing she does on this occasion can change their love. Mr. Jaggers, on the other hand, never tires of telling Pip that in their relationship he is acting purely as a businessman. Mr. Jaggers does not approve of the unknown benefactor's scheme and says so; he has no confidence that Pip will profit by his expectations and says so; he is simply carrying out instructions.

Life for Joe is a perpetual marrying and giving in marriage. He constantly gives his heart and accepts the mixed consequences of his generosity. Mr. Jaggers is the purest bachelor, the completely disassociated man. For him the world is a dungheap with an occasional jewel in it. The shrewd man rescues the jewels when he can; otherwise he tries to stay at a distance from the dungheap, and when he must touch it, as a criminal lawyer like Mr. Jaggers frequently must, he will constantly wash his hands with strong soap, as Mr. Jaggers does after each interview.

There are several curious things Dickens does with the characters of Joe and Mr. Jaggers. For one thing, they are both men, and for another they are both good men. More recent English novelists who have tried to defend the poetic view of experience ordinarily use a woman to embody it, and ordinarily make her superior to those who represent another view. . . .

But Dickens uses men to embody both the poetic and the analytic view of experience. Perhaps by the time he wrote

Great Expectations he no longer had much confidence in women as an embodiment of the poetic view; at least there are only two rather minor female characters in the whole book who are not cold and heartless. But, whatever the reason, by using male characters to embody both views, Dickens avoided the danger of allowing a question of truth to become a question of sex.

And it is testimony to Dickens' fairness that Mr. Jaggers is so powerful a character and so good a man. Some readers have not thought so well of him, but he seems to me to be admirable—honest, trustworthy, devoted to duty. In the end his way of looking at experience is mistaken, but he remains a good as well as a brilliant man, and in one wonderful scene he drops a hint that he knows his own mistake. . . .

THE MIXTURE OF GOOD AND EVIL

The plot of *Great Expectations* is a good one; it holds the reader's interest; it is full of surprises and odd turns; its complexities all come out neatly in the end. But more than that, it is a symbolic representation of Dickens' vision of the moral universe, and the chief characteristic of that vision is that good and evil, what we most desire and what we most loathe, are inextricably intertwined, involved with one another in such a way that no human hand can sort them out.

The plot is resolved through the discovery of a series of surprising relationships, and each of these is a relationship between something loathsome and something desirable. The first of these is the discovery that Pip does not owe his great expectations to the fairy godmother, Miss Havisham, but to the ogre, Magwitch. Magwitch has been transported to Australia; there he has prospered as a sheep rancher, and he has decided to use his wealth to make a gentleman of the little boy who stole the food and file for him on the marshes long ago. Pip's rise in the world has not been an act of magic; it has actually been a reward for theft, for what he has regarded as the most shameful deed of his life.

The second great discovery is that Estella, whom Pip has wasted his life in loving, is far from being a princess; she is in fact the illegitimate daughter of Magwitch by the criminal who now serves as Mr. Jaggers' servant. Miss Havisham is no fairy godmother; she is a foolish old meddler.

Life is not, Dickens is showing us symbolically by the plot, a dungheap in which one can find an occasional jewel to pluck out, as Mr. Jaggers supposes. It is an old, old growth; the fairest flower and the most noxious weed have their roots in the same ancient soil. Joe Gargery's view of experience is right because he has grasped this fact—not intellectually, for Joe is no intellectual, but by accepting in love the complexity of the moral universe. . . .

Pip himself represents an impure mixture of the easiest parts of both Joe's and Mr. Jaggers' attitudes toward experience.

Actually it is not altogether fair to compare Pip with Joe and Mr. Jaggers: they are unchanging, fixed points of reference in the book—so much so that they seem never to age. But Pip changes. When first we meet him he is an innocent little boy. When last we see him he is a man in early middle age, much chastened by experience. The book is essentially an account of Pip's moral education, and in order to understand the nature of that education we must see Pip's attitude toward experience clearly—in itself, and in relation to Joe's and Mr. Jaggers'.

Joe and Mr. Jaggers have this in common: they are both in some sense moral realists. To be sure, they differ as fundamentally as two men can about what should be dignified with the label of reality, but they are realists in that both accept the consequences of their own views. For Joe this means that, if to follow the demand of his heart, to love and cherish little Pip involves marrying a shrew, then he is ready to pay the price, and he never whines of it afterward. When Joe realizes that the larks that he and Pip were to share are never going to happen, when he realizes that there is no longer any place for him in Pip's life after Pip has gone to London, he recognizes the situation for what it is; his love takes on a tragic cast, but it remains love. Mr. Jaggers is equally steadfast in facing the worst that his own attitude toward life entails: he is a man isolated, cut off from other human beings—respected and feared but unloved. But Mr. Jaggers can face the worst, unflinching, and recognize it for what it is.

"AND THERE WAS I AGAIN!"

Pip differs from both men. He is not a realist; he is a fantasist. He supposes that he can have the best of both views and the unfavorable consequences of neither. He embraces isolation, as Mr. Jaggers does, but he embraces it selectively—

or, in other words, he becomes a terrible snob. He cuts himself off from his own past—he neglects Joe, he does not go back to the forge, he is ashamed of his blacksmith's arm among the languid or vicious young bloods whose society he cultivates in London. He isolates himself from those who love him, but he does not accept the natural consequence of his action, which is lovelessness. Love is as necessary to Pip as to Joe Gargery, but Pip wants it on his own terms, the terms of fantasy. He can only love the fairy-tale princess, the coldly glittering distant star, Estella.

Now Pip is not entirely to be blamed in all this. His early life *was* fantastic; his contacts with creatures like Magwitch and Miss Havisham could only encourage the habit of fantasy in him; and then in adolescence to have his wildest dreams realized, to be suddenly transformed from a humble village apprentice to a young Londoner with great expectations—what result could all this have except to make the boy suppose that the world is indeed whatever his fancy would like it to be? How could he avoid supposing that he was one singularly excused by the gods from facing consequences? . . .

The healing touch at the end of the novel is not the reunion of Pip and Estella, but Pip's return to the forge. By the time he goes back, his sister, Mrs. Joe Gargery, has long since died, and the ageless Joe has married Biddy, the girl whom Pip might once have married had he been free of the myth of his own life. They have a child, a little boy, and they have named him Pip. "And there was I again!" the old Pip cries to himself. Another generation has come along; another branch of that ancient vine, the human race, has sprung forth. Its roots are in the tangled dark, as ours are; they will have to learn to live with that fact, as we must; but perhaps, acknowledging the dark, they will do a better job of seeking the light.

Pip Unifies the Novel's Structure and Characters

Thomas Connolly

Most of Dickens's novels are long and loosely organized, but *Great Expectations* is more highly focused and compact. Thomas Connolly, professor emeritus at State University of New York, emphasizes these features in the three separate parts of the novel. Connolly points out that each of the three parts or stages has its own distinctive point of view: childhood (part 1), young manhood (part 2), and adulthood (part 3). And while there is a rich diversity of characters in the novel, all serve to further our understanding of Pip as he travels through these phases of life. As such, Pip is the common thread linking the separate parts of the novel, as well as the conduit through which all the characters flow.

In structure *Great Expectations* is notable among Dickens's works for its compression and the balanced proportion of its parts. It is exceptional, too, in its treatment of the [education] theme. It is natural in Dickens to find that the influencing factors which affect the life of the hero are outside the person himself. *Great Expectations* is no exception in this respect. However, in the earlier [education] novels—in *David Copperfield*, for example,—the hero emerges as essentially the same person who was introduced in the first pages of the novel. Spiritually he is relatively unchanged by these external forces, however much he may have prospered materially. But this is not true of Pip. He is altered in character by these forces, and it is this alteration which gives us the informing idea of the novel. Once this informing idea had been developed in the author's mind, the novel flowed structurally and thematically from it. The idea is, of course, the

Excerpted from "Technique in *Great Expectations*," by Thomas Connolly, *Philological Quarterly*, vol. 34, January 1955. Reprinted with the author's permission.

effect upon Pip's life of the lure of unearned money and false prosperity. It is not only, however, the story of one Philip Pirrip. Pip assumes a much larger role than that of an individual. . . . We must consider the story of Pip's life as a social criticism of the illusion of fortune which was sweeping society of the day into a whirlwind of falsity, sham, pretense, and social corruption. . . .

There is a wide variety of material present in *Great Expectations,* though it does not draw attention to itself because the various minor topics or themes are always carefully subordinated to the unity of the whole. The lengthy passages of social criticism which appeared in other novels are not to be found in this one. Each element of the action is made to carry the weight of the implicit theme of the novel. Hence, when Dickens introduces a minor theme, such as education (seen in the absurd school run by Mr. Wopsle's great aunt and in Mr. Pocket's tutoring system), it has no existence apart from the plot. It is all part of Pip's development and also part of the implicit social criticism that is his life. . . . Lurking over the entire work like a huge black spider which draws all threads of the material into a single, unified, web-like pattern, is the symbol of money. It is to money, either positively by acquisitiveness, or negatively by influence, that all persons and things in the novel are subject. . . .

CHILDHOOD

The point of view in *Great Expectations* is that of the first person, but it divides into three parts which correspond to the three structural parts of the novel.

Perhaps one of the greatest talents which Dickens possessed was that of accurate representation of the state of mind of childhood. In this part of his work there is usually none of the artificiality of Victorian convention which sometimes detracts from his representation of adult emotional life. The early chapters of this novel reveal Dickens's sympathy for and understanding of the psychology of childhood. The spirit of childhood experience is skilfully suggested in the scenes of Pip's theft of the food and his delivery of it to the convict. The childish mingling of emotions—generosity, pity, fear, guilt, and the belief in the omniscience of the adult world—is seen in the most perfect form. It reaches its peak in a weird flight of childish imagination when Pip comes upon the cattle on his way to the convict with the stolen food:

The mist was heavier yet when I got out upon the marshes, so that instead of my running at everything, everything seemed to run at me. This was very disagreeable to a guilty mind. The gates and dykes and banks came bursting at me through the mist, as if they cried as plainly as could be, "A boy with Somebody else's pork pie! Stop him!" The cattle came upon me with like suddenness, staring out of their eyes, and steaming out of their nostrils, "Halloa, young thief!" One black ox, with a white cravat on—who even had to my awakened conscience something of a clerical air—fixed me so obstinately with his eyes, and moved his blunt head round in such an accusatory manner as I moved round, that I blubbered out to him, "I couldn't help it, sir! It wasn't for myself I took it!" Upon which he put down his head, blew a cloud of smoke out of his nose, and vanished with a kick-up of his hind legs and a flourish of his tail.

It will be noticed that at the same time that this evocation of the childhood mood is accomplished, there is no departure from legitimate, cultured, adult language. The spirit of childhood has been generated and the adult language of the representation of that mood does not detract, generally, from the psychological effect. . . .

One other citation will be sufficient to demonstrate Dickens's understanding of child psychology and his achievement of the childish point of view. Upon his return from his first visit to Miss Havisham, Pip is cross-questioned by his sister and Pumblechook. In his fear of revealing the truth and his reluctance to satisfy their morbid curiosity, he resorts to sheer invention. The childish imagination is given free play to the obvious delight of the two examiners, who are willing to believe anything about the fantastic Miss Havisham. His inventions are really no more fantastic than the actuality, but to the childish mind they are more fascinating, and even Joe, who is so much a child himself in his simplicity, though disappointed by the fact that Pip lied, is much more upset when he discovers that there weren't any black coaches or huge dogs in the house. This resort to deception in dealing with an unsympathetic adult world is as natural to childhood as marble-playing and leap-frog.

YOUNG ADULTHOOD

In the second part of the novel the method of presentation becomes more complex. Here it is necessary to have Pip recount with true feeling and objectively the period of his illusions. To do this after the realization of the falseness and irony of the illusions, and still not to permit later disillusionment to be felt in the telling, is a difficult task. It is made more difficult by the absence of a third-person narrator to furnish the commentary. Dickens manages to give a true picture of Pip's priggishness and social vanity by the rigid suppression of anything which might resemble commentary on the part of the narrator. Had he permitted this to creep into Pip's narrative the effect would not have been nearly so striking as it is. The result amounts to tragic irony, the reproduction of the reality of an experience at a time when the realization of the folly of it is known. There is a doubleness of vision in those pages devoted to Joe's visit to Barnard's Inn in which both the cruelty and the horror of Pip's rejection and his realization of the full meaning of what he is doing become apparent.

Maturity

In the last part of the novel both childhood psychology and snobbish duality are left behind. Pip arrives at his final state of mind, and the resulting narration is much more simple. There is no childish distortion; there is no egotistical dislocation. Hence, melodrama replaces psychology in the reduction to essentials. The Magwitch escape plot, Compeyson's horrible death, Orlick's attempt on Pip's life, Miss Havisham's destruction, are all sheer melodrama and are all crowded into this last section. Disillusionment is the theme, but there is also the consolation of truth-facing in this final part. The novel ends sombrely, but the bitterness is relieved by the heightened melodramatic action.

Pip and Other Characters

In character development, too, *Great Expectations* represents a high point in Dickens's development. . . . Pip's character is traced in its development from boy to man. It is a full portrait. The reason for the realistic presentation of this hero is to be found in the fact that we are taken within the hero's mind. We are no longer external observers, left to judge the character of the observed solely from the evidence of his speech and actions. In presenting Pip, Dickens shows the detailed growth of a man from the internal vantage point of the man's own feelings. . . .

Herbert Pocket, Joe Gargery and Trabb's boy serve in varying degrees as norms against which Pip's life can be measured. Herbert has a duality of character, of which each half serves as a commentary on Pip. One side of his character is level, steady, and substantial. This is the Herbert who acts as Pip's social tutor, who comforts and cares for him when he has been injured, who is manager of the plans for Magwitch's escape. There is, however, another side of his nature which is similar to that second phase of Pip's life, the period of illusion. This is the Herbert who is even more outlandish in his expectations than Pip. This is the Herbert who is more hopelessly lost in his air castles because they have not even the insecure foundation of an unknown patron. According to Herbert, all he has to do to become an insurer of ships is to look about him for the necessary capital. The closest he comes to disillusionment is the realization "that an opening won't come to one, but one must go to it—so I have been." He has walked on 'Change during a busy time with a careful eye peeled for any capital that might come his way.

THE FOCUS ON PIP'S POINT OF VIEW

The 1947 film adaptation of Great Expectations, *starring John Mills and directed and cowritten by David Lean, is considered one of the most successful translations of a novel to the screen, as well as a film classic. Critic Carol MacKay emphasizes Lean's ability to re-create Pip's point of view in cinematic terms as the center of the film, just as it is in the novel.*

The screenwriters' major challenge and achievement lie in their handling of point of view. . . . From the outset, the film's narrator adopts Dickens' descriptions and conveys Pip's vulnerability; the post-production script in fact adds an overt link to the written page by stipulating an open book that provides the narrator's initial text. Another technique for entering Pip's mind . . . is the use of voice-overs—to express an imposed sense of guilt, to conjure up rationalizations, to echo phrases from Pip's past. But the most dramatic translation of viewpoint is definitely a visual matter: it develops from a subjective camera that uses eye-level shots to express the young Pip's fear of the adult world and that creates a sustained series of images to convey Pip's feverish delirium after Magwitch's death (this last sequence approaches montage, almost transposing the pictures that earlier flood Pip's mind when he is Orlick's prisoner).

Carol Hanbery MacKay, "A Novel's Journey into Film: The Case of *Great Expectations,*" *Literature/Film Quarterly* 13 (1985), pp. 127–34.

This is the Herbert whom Pip rescues in the one decent act of his period of snobbery. Had there been no Pip to save him with the actuality of a partnership, Herbert would have remained in his world of illusion.

Joe Gargery, in a different fashion, also serves as a commentary on Pip. He is a recurrence of the Dickens "good" earthy character. He represents in one human frame all the best elements of human nature. When he appears in Pip's rooms he becomes the most damning evidence of Pip's degeneration. The irony of the rejection is made all the more evident by Joe's consciousness of the system of social stratification. "Diwisions among such must come, and must be met as they come." It is the fatalistic acceptance which points up the evil of the system.

Trabb's boy is almost pure demon. He is a demon who serves a delightful purpose, and I can conceive of no reader who does not feel like cheering him on as he capers on High Street and, shred by shred, strips Pip down to the disgusting bone. To make him "the joy of life felt by those who have nothing else but life," as Chesterton does, is to stretch him a little beyond his capacity. Humphry House has summarized his role and character quite well:

> As things were he was a good pin to prick Pip's conceit; but if he himself had come into a fortune, he would have been just as nasty about it as Pip in his own way; and his way might have been worse.[1]

Jaggers, Wemmick, Magwitch, Wopsle, Pumblechook, Belinda Pocket, Matthew Pocket and Biddy are all interesting and well-drawn characters whose casual listing should in no way imply that they are not each worth a serious and detailed investigation. They all show the extent to which Dickens had advanced in character delineation. In *Great Expectations* almost no character serves but a single purpose. Dickens had learned how to make his characters complex so that they function economically both in the basic plot and in the thematic presentation. *Great Expectations* is a novel which treats the social fable in terms of the life of one man. A wealth of material and characterization is present in the work, but it is so closely controlled by the author that no individual element or part exists which does not carry its proportionate share of the main plot and theme.

---

1. Humphry House, *The Dickens World* (London, 1941), p. 159

Pip's Bought Self

Pam Morris

Pam Morris, who earned her doctorate in literature at Edinburgh University, shows how Pip's rise in social status is a matter of things bought with money, linking him to our contemporary notion of conspicuous consumption and making him "the first representation of the yuppie in fiction." Pip's growing debts indicate the falseness of his gentility, and when Magwitch reveals himself as Pip's benefactor, Pip is brought down to the reality of his low social status. Morris asserts that Magwitch's character demonstrates the deep connections between crime and the wealth of the upper class. And although criminality observes no class boundaries, she does make a distinction between the poor's "crimes of need" and the wealthy's "crimes of greed."

Pip is shown to mark his changed expectations by a metamorphosis of self-image. He orders himself a 'fashionable suit of clothes', 'an article much in vogue among the nobility and gentry'. So he begins to construct the appropriate style of wealth. Indeed, the only employment of Pip as gentleman offered by the narrative account is that of conspicuous consumption and display. The studies with Mr Pocket are never detailed, but reader attention is frequently called to descriptions of lifestyle. His rooms are luxuriously furnished, his personal appearance enhanced by jewellery, his status advertized by the canary livery of the Avenger, and his reputation confirmed by membership of a fashionable club. Pip as character is shown to become a gentleman by assuming the style of wealth. This is probably the first representation of the yuppie in fiction. What this constructs is a life of surface, a consumerist perception of self as bought. The [contrast] to this within the text is Wemmick's inventive pleasure in a self-made domestic lifestyle whose gadgets are all intended to enhance connection by breaching [his old father's] isolating deafness. 'I am my own engineer, and my own plumber, and my own gardener' he is presented as telling Pip.

In Pip's case, even the bought style is based upon growing debts, and this in turn is based upon false expectations. The whole existence as gentleman is represented in the text as a falsification and a counterfeiting of self. The fairytale form of transformation into prince reverses over into the curse of stolen or enchanted identity. The adult narrator names himself with the deep bitterness of loss a 'self-swindler', cheating himself with 'spurious coin' of his own making. There is a sad diminishment in the movement of the narrative from that initial fairytale invocation of transformation and celebration in terms of golden dishes and velvet coaches to the representation of Pip's empty pretence of plenitude in London, that 'gay fiction among us that we were all constantly enjoying ourselves, and a skeleton truth that we never did'. Despite its fictionality the process of genteel restyling is depicted as devoid of imagination. Pip's capacity for playfulness died at Satis House. The text presents his transformation into gentleman as merely a matter of buying the appropriate style of display. . . . The spectacle of wealthy style as presented in Pip as character is intended to intimidate those it separates off as 'common', and it counterfeits self in a bought image. As gentleman, Pip fully reveals that to 'Hav-is-sham'. This falsification of self is appropriately articulated in the parodic mirroring of Pip's pretensions by Trabb's boy, a wonderful re-invention of the urchin: 'Don't know yah, don't know yah, pon my soul don't know yah!'

This imagery of shamming, counterfeiting, or forging is the master trope of the text, locking together the interconnection of money with criminality. Almost all the crime mentioned in the story is of coining, forging, or swindling. Jaggers is even said to keep a smelter on the premises. The whole system of law, as represented in the novel, is implicated in a pervasive network of counterfeiting. Witnesses are paid to 'sham' respectability, innocence is bought from the lawyer best able to construct its appearance. Underlying this forgery of justice by money, is subservience to style. The *Westminster Review*, in writing about the 'gigantic system of dishonesty' running beneath 'our whole social fabric', concluded, 'we are all implicated . . . Scarcely a man is to be found who would not behave with more civility to a knave in broadcloth than to a knave in fustian'. The account of Magwitch's trial provides a fictional exposure of this use of money to construct the style of respectability and lawfulness.

MAGWITCH'S DEAR BOY

In 1860, *The Times* described the plight of children orphaned or 'turned out of doors [to] become what are called Arabs of the streets. They have not a hope or a thought but of mendicacy or robbery . . . in the streets, in the school of crime, and on the way to prison, or the penal settlement' (August 15, 1860). This is a real-life version of the fictional story of Magwitch: 'In jail and out of jail . . . carted here and carted there . . . tramping, begging, thieving, working sometimes when I could'. In the speech image of Magwitch the text constructs a powerful and passionate voice to represent the silenced and criminalized poor. . . . Magwitch's character discourse is dominated by an urge for reconnection. While the speech image of Pip as gentleman struggles to defend a sense of separation and differentiation, Magwitch's reiterated interpellation of him as 'dear boy' seeks to pull him into a recognition of affection and intimacy—a 'commonness' which he dreads. The representation of Magwitch's physical gestures, too, stress the impulse to make fellowship material in actual bodily contact. In detailing Pip's shuddering reaction, narrative discourse most powerfully recreates the repugnance and shrinking of the prosperous from the physical reality of those Lord Shaftesbury described as so 'filthy' and 'ill-clad' that they only 'creep forth' at night. The representation of the fairytale sham of fashionable style is shattered by . . . contact with the intensity conveyed of Magwitch as a physical bodily presence—this is a triumph of the novel's mimetic [imitative] realism. Once returned, the immediacy and passion of this physical challenge to a counterfeit reality can no longer be pushed from consciousness: 'everything in him that it was most desirable to repress, started through that thin layer of pretence, and seemed to come blazing out at the crown of his head'. The energy of the verbs here seems to deny the possibility of any further containment.

THE CONNECTION BETWEEN CRIMINALITY AND WEALTH

However, Magwitch, too, is represented as having bought the consumer dream. His discourse lovingly recognizes and catalogues the items of Pip's fashionable lifestyle: lodgings 'fit for a lord', gold and diamond rings, fine linen, books. But Magwitch's discourse overtly connects this consumer desire to the lack which makes its idealized images so impelling to the poor and outcast—the need to escape from a self-image perceived as low or contemptible. 'And then, dear boy, it was a recompense to me, look'ee here, to know in secret that I was making a gentleman'. Even a vicarious investment in wealthy style offers defence in phantasy against interpellation as an 'ignorant common fellow', as Bagehot recognized when he described the 'charmed spectacle of society' as 'imposing on the many and guiding their fancies as it will'. Royalty, joined now by various 'stars', constructed, like Estella, as objects of desire, offer that same vicarious and consoling identification with glamour to those unlikely ever to share it, articulated in the character discourse of Magwitch. More importantly, his speech reconnects wealthy lifestyle and conspicuous consumption to the reality of their source in degraded and punishing labour. 'I lived rough, that you should live smooth, I worked hard, that you should be above work'. Those words, in their starkness, lay bare the exploitative chain of connection structuring the economic inequality of class. This is always the uncomfortable truth repressed and excluded from the fascinating spectacle of wealth.

"CRIMES OF NEED" VERSUS "CRIMES OF GREED"

Pip, like the prosperous in the real world, is represented as inscribing the space of this repressed knowledge with criminality: 'In the dreadful mystery that he was to me . . . I would sit and look at him, wondering what he had done, and loading him with all the crimes in the Calendar'. Pip even mimics the urge to incarcerate the poor, locking Magwitch into his room at night. However, the text does not sanction this recontainment. Magwitch's first person account of his life constructs the criminalized poor, not as object of knowledge, but as passionately knowing subject whose discourse reconnects the link between common needs and 'crimes' of want. . . . The language of Magwitch, in *Great Expectations*, asserts the simple compulsion of hunger: 'What the Devil was I to do? I must put something into my stomach, mustn't I?' The laws of property cannot bind those denied work, food, and shelter. In addition, Magwitch's discourse functions to expose the chain of connection between crimes of need and crimes of greed. Even a slight disturbance of the labour market, *The Times* disclosed, could reduce men and women to starvation and beggary. This level of common need pushed the poor, like Magwitch, into the power of those, like Compeyson, involved in crimes of swindling and fraud, not in order to stay alive, but to indulge the cultivated needs of wealthy lifestyle. The chains of social interconnection as represented in *Great Expectations* are altogether harsh and sinister. . . .

Pip's Moral Journey

G. Robert Stange

Prominent literary critic G. Robert Stange was for many years a professor of English at the University of Minnesota. Focusing on Pip's relationship with Magwitch, Stange sees a clearly defined morality in Pip's experience. In his initial innocence and goodness, Pip makes a moral connection with the suffering convict. But as he becomes more cosmopolitan and aware of the world, Pip becomes morally confused. This is clearly shown when he spurns humble Joe's warmth in pursuit of proud Estella's coldness and when he hides his relationship with Magwitch. Pip's arrogance and charitable emptiness leave him bereft and immoral, after which he can begin to be "cleansed." He finally recognizes his selfishness as a symptom of a diseased soul; and his long illness that follows symbolizes the death of this old egoism. Likewise, Pip's humility before Magwitch and Joe in the final third of the novel represents a moral reawakening, a return of the sympathetic boy on the marsh of so many years ago.

Great Expectations is conceived as a moral fable; it is the story of a young man's development from the moment of his first self-awareness, to that of his mature acceptance of the human condition.

So natural a theme imposes an elemental form on the novel: the over-all pattern is defined by the process of growth, and Dickens employs many of the motifs of folklore. The story of Pip falls into three phases which clearly display a dialectic progression. We see the boy first in his natural condition in the country, responding and acting instinctively and therefore virtuously. The second stage of his career involves a negation of child-like simplicity; Pip acquires his "expectations," renounces his origins, and moves to the city.

Excerpted from "Expectations Well Lost: Dickens' Fable for His Time," by G. Robert Stange, *College English*, vol. 17, October 1954, pp. 9–17.

He rises in society, but since he acts through calculation rather than through instinctive charity, his moral values deteriorate as his social graces improve. This middle phase of his career culminates in a sudden fall, the beginning of a redemptive suffering which is dramatically concluded by an attack of brain fever leading to a long coma. It is not too fanciful to regard this illness as a symbolic death; Pip rises from it regenerate and percipient. In the final stage of growth he returns to his birthplace, abandons his false expectations, accepts the limitations of his condition, and achieves a partial synthesis of the virtue of his innocent youth and the melancholy insight of his later experience. . . .

Pip's career is a parable which illustrates several religious paradoxes: he can gain only by losing all he has; only by being defiled can he be cleansed. Magwitch returns to claim his gentleman, and finally the convict's devotion and suffering arouse Pip's charity; by the time Magwitch has been captured and is dying Pip has accepted him and come to love him as a true father. The relationship is the most important one in the novel: in sympathizing with Magwitch Pip assumes the criminal's guilt; in suffering with and finally loving the despised and rejected man he finds his own real self.

Magwitch did not have to learn to love Pip. He was naturally devoted to "the small bundle of shivers," the outcast boy who brought him the stolen food and the file in the misty graveyard. There is a natural bond, Dickens suggests, between the child and the criminal; they are alike in their helplessness; both are repressed and tortured by established society, and both rebel against its incomprehensible authority. In the first scene Magwitch forces Pip to commit his first "criminal" act, to steal the file and food from his sister's house. Though this theft produces agonies of guilt in Pip, we are led to see it not as a sin but as an instinctive act of mercy. Magwitch, much later, tells Pip: "I first become aware of myself, down in Essex, a thieving turnips for my living." Dickens would have us, in some obscure way, conceive the illicit act as the means of self-realization.

In the opening section of the novel the view moves back and forth between the escaped criminal on the marshes and the harsh life in the house of Pip's sister, Mrs. Joe Gargery. The "criminality" of Pip and the convict is contrasted with the socially approved cruelty and injustice of Mrs. Joe and her respectable friends. The elders who come to the Christmas feast at the Gargerys' are pleased to describe Pip as a criminal: the young are, according to Mr. Hubble, "naterally wicious." During this most bleak of Christmas dinners the child is treated not only as outlaw, but as animal. In Mrs. Joe's first speech Pip is called a "young monkey"; then, as the spirits of the revellers rise, more and more comparisons are made between boys and animals. Uncle Pumblechook, devouring his pork, toys with the notion of Pip's having been born a "Squeaker":

> "If you had been born such, would you have been here now? Not you. . . .
>
> "Unless in that form," said Mr. Wopsle, nodding towards the dish.
>
> "But I don't mean in that form, sir," returned Mr. Pumblechook, who had an objection to being interrupted; "I mean, enjoying himself with his elders and betters, and improving himself with their conversation, and rolling in the lap of luxury. Would he have been doing that? No, he wouldn't. And what would have been your destination?" turning on me again. "You would have been disposed of for so many shillings according to the market price of the article, and Dunstable the butcher would have come up to you as you lay in your straw, and he would have whipped you under his left arm, and with his right he would have tucked up his frock to get a penknife from out of his waistcoat-pocket, and he would have shed your blood and had your life. No bringing up by hand then. Not a bit of it!"

This identification of animal and human is continually repeated in the opening chapters of the novel, and we catch its resonance throughout the book. When the two convicts—Pip's "friend" and the other fugitive, Magwitch's ancient enemy—are captured, we experience the horror of official justice, which treats the prisoners as if they were less than human: "No one seemed surprised to see him, or interested in seeing him, or glad to see him, or sorry to see him, or spoke a word, except that somebody in the boat growled as if to dogs, 'Give way, you!'" And the prison ship, lying beyond the mud of the shore, looked to Pip "like a wicked Noah's ark."

The theme of this first section of the novel—which concludes with the capture of Magwitch and his return to the prison ship—might be called "the several meanings of humanity." Only the three characters who are in some way social outcasts–Pip, Magwitch, and Joe Gargery the childlike blacksmith—act in charity and respect the humanity of others. To Magwitch Pip is distinctly not an animal, and

not capable of adult wickedness: "You'd be but a fierce young
hound indeed, if at your time of life you could help to hunt a
wretched warmint." And when, after he is taken, the convict
shields Pip by confessing to have stolen the Gargerys' pork
pie, Joe's absolution affirms the dignity of man:

> "God knows you're welcome to it—so far as it was ever
> mine," returned Joe, with a saving remembrance of Mrs. Joe.
> "We don't know what you have done, but we wouldn't have
> you starved to death for it, poor miserable fellow-creatur.—
> Would us, Pip?"

CHILDHOOD BETRAYED

The next section of the narrative is less tightly conceived
than the introductory action. Time is handled loosely; Pip
goes to school, and becomes acquainted with Miss Havisham of Satis House and the beautiful Estella. The section
concludes when Pip has reached early manhood, been told
of his expectations, and has prepared to leave for London.
These episodes develop, with variations, the theme of childhood betrayed. Pip himself renounces his childhood by coming to accept the false social values of middle-class society.
His perverse development is expressed by persistent images
of the opposition between the human and the non-human,
the living and the dead. . . .

From his visits to Satis House Pip acquires his false admiration for the genteel; he falls in love with Estella and fails
to see that she is the cold instrument of Miss Havisham's revenge on human passion and on life itself. When Pip learns
he may expect a large inheritance from an unknown source
he immediately assumes (incorrectly) that Miss Havisham is
his benefactor; she does not undeceive him. Money, which
is also death, is appropriately connected with the old lady
rotting away in her darkened room.

Conflicting values in Pip's life are also expressed by the
opposed imagery of stars and fire. Estella is by name a star,
and throughout the novel stars are conceived as pitiless:
"And then I looked at the stars, and considered how awful it
would be for a man to turn his face up to them as he froze to
death, and see no help or pity in all the glittering multitude."
Estella and her light are described as coming down the dark
passage of Satis House "like a star," and when she has become a woman she is constantly surrounded by the bright
glitter of jewelry.

Joe Gargery, on the other hand, is associated with the warm fire of the hearth or forge. It was his habit to sit and rake the fire between the lower bars of the kitchen grate, and his workday was spent at the forge. The extent to which Dickens intended the contrast between the warm and the cold lights—the vitality of Joe and the frigid glitter of Estella—is indicated in a passage that describes the beginnings of Pip's disillusionment with his expectations:

> When I woke up in the night . . . I used to think, with a weariness on my spirits, that I should have been happier and better if I had never seen Miss Havisham's face, and had risen to manhood content to be partners with Joe in the honest old forge. Many a time of an evening, when I sat alone looking at the fire, I thought, after all, there was no fire like the forge fire and the kitchen fire at home.

> Yet Estella was so inseparable from all my restlessness and disquiet of mind, that I really fell into confusion as to the limits of my own part in its production.

At the end of the novel Pip finds the true light on the homely hearth, and in a last twist of the father-son theme, Joe emerges as a true parent—the only kind of parent that Dickens could ever fully approve, one that remains a child. The moral of this return to Joe sharply contradicts the accepted picture of Dickens as a radical critic of society: Joe is a humble countryman who is content with the place in the social order he has been appointed to fulfill. He fills it "well and with respect"; Pip learns that he can do no better than to emulate him. . . .

ACCEPTING COMMON GUILT

The final moral vision of *Great Expectations* has to do with the nature of sin and guilt. After visiting Newgate Pip, still complacent and self-deceived, thinks how strange it was that he should be encompassed by the taint of prison and crime. He tries to beat the prison dust off his feet and to exhale its air from his lungs; he is going to meet Estella, who must not be contaminated by the smell of crime. Later it is revealed that Estella, the pure, is the bastard child of Magwitch and a murderess. Newgate is figuratively described as a greenhouse, and the prisoners as plants carefully tended by Wemmick, assistant to Mr. Jaggers. These disturbing metaphors suggest that criminality is the condition of life. Dickens would distinguish between the native, inherent sinfulness from which men can be redeemed, and that evil which destroys life: the sin of the hypocrite or oppressor, the smothering wickedness of corrupt institutions. The last stage of Pip's progression is reached when he learns to love the criminal and to accept his own implication in the common guilt.

Though Dickens' interpretation is theologically heterodox, he deals conventionally with the ancient question of free will and predestination. In one dramatic paragraph Pip's "fall" is compared with the descent of the rock slab on the sleeping victim in the Arabian Nights tale: Slowly, slowly, "all the work, near and afar, that tended to the end, had been accomplished; and in an instant the blow was struck, and the roof of my stronghold dropped upon me." Pip's fall was the result of a chain of predetermined events but he was, nevertheless, responsible for his own actions; toward the end of the novel Miss Havisham gravely informs him: "You have made your own snares. I never made them."

Parallels Between Pip, Orlick, and Drummle

Julian Moynahan

In one of the most famous and influential critical studies of *Great Expectations,* Julian Moynahan, professor emeritus of literature at Rutgers University, focuses on two minor characters who assume major importance in the context of Pip's psychological situation: Dolge Orlick and Bentley Drummle. Pip is abused by Mrs. Joe and Estella, and each of them in turn suffers: Mrs. Joe is murdered by Orlick, and Estella is beaten by Drummle. Thus Orlick and Drummle act out Pip's revenge, even if he does not consciously direct it. In the case of Mrs. Joe, he does feel consciously guilty. Miss Havisham, a third abuser of Pip, later accidentally burns to death. Moynahan argues interestingly that it is as if Pip's psychology lights the fire.

I would suggest that Orlick rather than Magwitch is the figure from the criminal milieu of the novel whose relations to him come to define Pip's implicit participation in the acts of violence with which the novel abounds. Considered by himself, Orlick is a figure of melodrama. He is unmotivated, his origins are shrouded in mystery, his violence is unqualified by regret. In this last respect he is the exact opposite of Pip, who is, of course, filled with regret whenever he remembers how he has neglected his old friends at the forge.

On the other hand, if we consider Orlick in his connections with Pip, some rather different observations can be made. In the first place, there is a peculiar parallel between the careers of the two characters. We first encounter Orlick as he works side by side with Pip at the forge. Circumstances also cause them to be associated in the assault on Mrs. Joe. Orlick strikes the blow, but Pip feels, with some justification,

Excerpted from "The Hero's Guilt: The Case of *Great Expectations*," by Julian Moynahan, *Essays in Criticism*, vol. 10, no. 1, January 1960, pp. 60–79. Reprinted with permission of the author.

that he supplied the assault weapon. Pip begins to develop his sense of alienation from the village after he has been employed by Miss Havisham to entertain her in her house. But Orlick too turns up later on working for Miss Havisham as gatekeeper. Finally, after Pip has become a partisan of the convict, it turns out that Orlick also has become a partisan of an ex-convict, Compeyson, who is Magwitch's bitter enemy.

Up to a point, Orlick seems not only to dog Pip's footsteps, but also to present a parody of Pip's upward progress through the novel, as though he were in competitive pursuit of some obscene great expectations of his own. Just as Pip centres his hopes successively on the forge, Satis House, and London, so Orlick moves his base of operations successively from the forge, to Satis House, and to London. From Pip's point of view, Orlick has no right to interest himself in any of the people with whom Pip has developed close ties. For instance, he is appalled when he discovers that his tender feeling for Biddy is given a distorted echo by Orlick's obviously lecherous interest in the same girl. And when he discovers that Orlick has the right of entry into Satis House he warns Jaggers to advise Miss Havisham to get rid of him. But somehow he cannot keep Orlick out of his affairs. When Magwitch appears at Pip's London lodging half-way through the novel, Orlick is crouching in darkness on the landing below Pip's apartment. And when Pip is about to launch the escape attempt down the Thames, his plans are frustrated by the trick which brings him down to the marshes to face Orlick in the hut by the limekiln. Its lurid melodrama and the awkwardness of its integration with the surrounding narrative has made many readers dismiss this scene as a piece of popular writing aimed at the less intelligent members of Dickens's audience. But the confrontation of Orlick and Pip on the marshes is crucial for an understanding of the problem I am discussing, because it is the scene in which Dickens comes closest to making explicit the analogy between the hero and the novel's principal villain and criminal.

Orlick inveigles Pip to the limepit not only to kill him but to overwhelm him with accusations. Addressing Pip over and over again as 'Wolf', an epithet he might more readily apply to himself, he complains that Pip has cost him his place, come between him and a young woman in whom he was interested, tried to drive him out of the country, and been a perpetual obstacle in the path of his own uncouth ambitions. But the charge he makes with the greatest force and conviction is that Pip bears the final responsibility for the assault on Mrs. Joe:

> 'I tell you it was your doing—I tell you it was done through you,' he retorted, catching up the gun and making a blow with the stock at the vacant air between us. 'I come upon her from behind, as I come upon you to-night. I giv' it to her! I left her for dead, and if there had been a limekiln as nigh her as there is now nigh you, she shouldn't have come to life again. But it warn't old Orlick as did it; it was you. You was favoured, and he was bullied and beat. Old Orlick bullied and beat, eh? Now you pays for it. You done it; now you pays for it.'

The entire scene was a nightmare quality. This is at least partly due to the weird reversal of rôles, by which the innocent figure is made the accused and the guilty one the accuser. As in a dream the situation is absurd, yet like a dream it may contain hidden truth. On the one hand Orlick, in interpreting Pip's character, seems only to succeed in describing himself—ambitious, treacherous, murderous, and without compunction. On the other hand, several of Orlick's charges are justified, and it is only in the assumption that Pip's motives are as black as his own that he goes wrong. We know, after all, that Pip is ambitious, and that he has repudiated his early associates as obstacles to the fulfilment of his genteel aspirations. Another interesting observation can be made about Orlick's charge that 'it was you as did for your shrew sister'. Here Orlick presents Pip as the responsible agent, himself merely as the weapon. But this is an exact reversal of Pip's former assumptions about the affair. All in all, Orlick confronts the hero in this scene, not merely as would-be murderer, but also as a distorted and darkened mirror-image. In fact, he presents himself as a monstrous caricature of the tender-minded hero, insisting that they are two of a kind with the same ends, pursued through similarly predatory and criminal means. This is what his wild accusations come down to. . . .

A DANGEROUS YOUNG MAN?

We might begin with the apparently cynical remark that Pip, judged on the basis of what happens to many of the characters closely associated with him, is a very dangerous young man. He is not accident-prone, but a great number of people who move into his orbit decidedly are. Mrs. Joe is bludgeoned, Miss Havisham goes up in flames, Estella is exposed through her rash marriage to vaguely specified tortures at the hands of her brutal husband, Drummle. Pumblechook has his house looted and his mouth stuffed with flowering annuals by a gang of thieves led by Orlick. All of these characters, with the exception of Estella, stand at one time or another in the relation of patron, patroness, or authority-figure to Pip the boy or Pip the man. (Pumblechook is, of course, a parody patron, and his comic chastisement is one of the most satisfying things in the book.) Furthermore, all of these characters, including Estella, have hurt, humiliated, or thwarted Pip in some important way. All in some way have stood between him and the attainment of the full measure of his desires. All are punished.

Let us group these individual instances. Mrs. Joe, the cruel foster-mother, and Pumblechook, her approving and hypocritical relation by marriage, receive their punishment from the hands of Orlick. Mrs. Joe hurts Pip and is hurt in turn by Orlick. Pip has the motive of revenge—a lifetime of brutal beatings and scrubbings inflicted by his sister—but Orlick, a journeyman who does not even lodge with the Gargerys, bludgeons Mrs. Joe after she has provoked a quarrel between him and his master. If we put together his relative lack of motive with his previously quoted remarks at the limekiln and add to these Pip's report of his own extraordinary reaction upon first hearing of the attack—

> With my head full of George Barnwell, I was at first disposed to believe that *I* must have had some hand in the attack upon my sister, or at all events that as her near relation, popularly known to be under obligations to her, I was a more legitimate object of suspicion than anyone else—

we arrive at an anomalous situation which can best be resolved on the assumption that Orlick acts merely as Pip's punitive instrument or weapon.

With regard to Pumblechook's chastisement, the most striking feature is not that Orlick should break into a house, but that he should break into Pumblechook's house. Why not Trabb's? One answer might be that Trabb has never stood in Pip's light. Pumblechook's punishment is nicely proportioned to his nuisance value for Pip. Since he has never succeeded in doing him any great harm with his petty slanders, he escapes with a relatively light wound. Although we are told near the end of the novel that Orlick was caught and jailed after the burglary, we are never told that Pip reported

Orlick's murderous assault on him or his confessions of his assault on Mrs. Joe to the police. Despite the fact that there is enough accumulated evidence to hang him, Orlick's end is missing from the book. Actually, it seems that Orlick simply evaporates into thin air after his punitive rôle has been performed. His case needs no final disposition because he has only existed, essentially, as an aspect of the hero's own far more problematic case.

ESTELLA'S PUNISHMENT

Estella receives her chastisement at the hands of Bentley Drummle. How does this fit into the pattern we have been exploring? In the first place, it can be shown that Drummle stands in precisely the same analogical relationship to Pip as Orlick does. Drummle is a reduplication of Orlick at a point higher on the social-economic scale up which Pip moves with such rapidity through the first three-quarters of the novel. Drummle, like Orlick, is a criminal psychopath. At Jaggers's dinner party the host, a connoisseur of criminal types, treats Drummle as 'one of the true sort', and Drummle demonstrates how deserving he is of this distinction when he tries to brain the harmless Startop with a heavy tumbler.

But the most impressive evidence that Orlick and Drummle are functional equivalents is supplied by the concrete particulars of their description. To an extraordinary degree, these two physically powerful, inarticulate, and dark-complexioned villains are presented to the reader in terms more often identical than similar. Orlick, again and again, is one who lurks and lounges, Drummle is one who lolls and lurks. When Pip, Startop, and Drummle go out rowing, the last 'would always creep in-shore like some uncomfortable amphibious creature, even when the tide would have sent him fast on his way; and I always think of him as coming after us in the dark or by the back-water, when our own two boats were breaking the sunset or the moonlight in mid-stream'. When Startop walks home after Jaggers's party, he is followed by Drummle but on the opposite side of the street, 'in the shadow of the houses, much as he was wont to follow in his boat'. The other creeper, follower and amphibian of *Great Expectations* is Orlick, whose natural habitat is the salt marsh, who creeps his way to the dark landing below Pip's apartment to witness the return of Magwitch from abroad, who creeps behind Biddy and Pip as they walk conversing on the marshes and overhears Pip say he will do anything to drive Orlick from the neighbourhood, who appears out of the darkness near the turnpike house on the night Pip returns from Pumblechook's to discover that his sister has been assaulted, and who, finally, creeps his way so far into Pip's private business that he ends by acting as agent for Compeyson, Magwitch's—and Pip's—shadowy antagonist.

Like Orlick, Drummle is removed from the action suddenly; Pip is given no opportunity to settle old and bitter scores with him. In the last chapter we hear that he is dead 'from an accident consequent on ill-treating a horse'. This is the appropriate end for a sadist whose crimes obviously included wife-beating. But more important to the present argument is our recognition that Drummle has been employed to break a woman who had, in the trite phrase, broken Pip's heart. Once he has performed his function as Pip's vengeful surrogate he can be assigned to the fate he so richly deserves.

Mrs. Joe beats and scrubs Pip until she is struck down by heavy blows on the head and spine. Pumblechook speaks his lies about him until his mouth is stuffed with flowers. Estella treats his affections with cold contempt until her icy pride is broken by a brutal husband. In this series Orlick and Drummle behave far more like instruments of vengeance than like three-dimensional characters with understandable grudges of their own. In terms of my complete argument, they enact an aggressive potential that the novel defines, through patterns of analogy and linked resemblances, as belonging in the end to Pip and to his unconscionably ambitious hopes.

REVENGE ON MISS HAVISHAM

When Miss Havisham bursts into flames, there is no Orlick or Drummle in the vicinity to be accused of having set a match to her. In the long series of violence which runs through *Great Expectations* from the beginning to end, this is one climax of violence that can be construed as nothing more than accidental. And yet it is an accident which Pip, on two occasions, has foreseen. Before Miss Havisham burns under the eye of the horror-struck hero, she has already come to a violent end twice in his hallucinated fantasies—in Pip's visionary experiences in the abandoned brewery, where he sees Miss Havisham hanging by the neck from a beam. He has this vision once as a child, on the occasion of his first visit to Satis House, and once as an adult, on the occasion on his last visit, just a few minutes before Miss Havisham's accident occurs. What are we to make, if anything, of these peculiar hallucinatory presentiments and of the coincidence by which they come true?

The child first sees his patroness hanging from a beam after his first hour of service with her. At this point the novel dwells at length on his keen awareness that he has been cruelly treated, generalises on the extreme sensitiveness of children to injustice, and describes how Pip in utter frustration vents his injured feelings by kicking a wall and twisting his own hair. In these passages it seems to me that the reader is being prepared to interpret Pip's immediately ensuing hallucination as the child's further attempt to discharge his anger and grief against his adult tormenter. In fantasy Pip punishes a woman whom in fact he cannot disturb in any way, and, by hanging her, attempts to destroy the threat to his peace and security which she represents. This interpretation excludes the possibility of a supernatural element in the experience; the novel provides abundant evidence that the imagination of a child operating under a great stress of emotion is possessed of a hallucinatory power. When Pip carries stolen provisions to Magwitch on the marshes, his guilt-ridden imagination effects a transformation of the countryside through which he passes, until even gates, dykes, banks, cattle and a signpost seem to him to be pursuing him and crying out his guilt. Pip's hallucination, then, is an imaginative fantasy which both projects and disguises the boy's desire to punish his employer and to destroy her baleful power over him.

Pip experiences no recurrence of the hallucination during the long years of an association with Miss Havisham based on his mistaken assumption that she is the sole author of his good fortunes. The fantasy returns only after his eyes have been opened to the fact that nothing has come to him from Miss Havisham except unhappiness. On that last visit to Satis House he learns definitely of Estella's marriage. With this information the last link between him and his former employer snaps. The false fairy godmother kneels to ask forgiveness for her crimes against him, and the duped hero offers forgiveness sincerely, if sadly. Nevertheless, as Pip strolls through the ruins of the estate he is not able to refrain from brooding over Miss Havisham's 'profound unfitness for this earth', and when he walks into the chilly, twilit brewery building he is not able to prevent the return of the old hallucination of Miss Havisham hanging from the beam. We are told that this was owing to the revival of a childish association. But surely the episode represents more than a curious psychological detail. It is profoundly right that the fantasy should return at a time when he can see in complete clarity and detail how his connection with Miss Havisham has hurt him. It is profoundly right that he should forgive the false patroness and yet not forgive her, behave generously toward her and yet feel deeply that she has no right to live, treat her with some degree of melancholy affection, yet hate her also in the depths of his being.

We need not deny Dickens the insight necessary to the imagining of so ambivalent a response in the hero of his great novel. And we should not commit the anachronism of demanding that this response be defined in the novel analytically and self-consciously—that the hero should tell us, 'I forgave Miss Havisham as fully as I could, but continued to think how well it would have been for me if she had never set foot on this earth.' Pip's ambivalence is embodied dramatically. It must be known not as it is talked about, but as enacted. A man forgives a woman, then hallucinates her death by hanging. A man watches a woman burst into flames, then leaps bravely to her rescue, but in the course of describing this rescue is forced to remark, 'We were on the ground struggling like desperate enemies.'

A MURDERER'S GUILT

How do these hallucinations, the second followed immediately by Miss Havisham's fatal accident, add to the burden of the hero's guilt? The answer is obvious. Because Pip's destructive fantasy comes true in reality, he experiences the equivalent of a murderer's guilt. As though he had the evil eye, or as though there were more than a psychological truth in the old cliché, 'if looks could kill', Pip moves from the brewery, where he has seen Miss Havisham hanging, to the door of her room, where he gives her one long, last look—until she is consumed by fire. But here the psychological truth suffices to establish imaginative proof that Pip can no more escape untainted from his relationship to the former patroness than he can escape untainted from any of his relationships to characters who have held and used the power to destroy or hamper his ambitious struggles. In all these relationships the hero becomes implicated in violence. With Estella, Pumblechook, and Mrs. Joe, the aggressive drive is enacted by surrogates linked to the hero himself by ties of analogy. With Miss Havisham the surrogate is missing. Miss Havisham falls victim to the purely accidental. But the 'impurity' of Pip's motivation, as it is revealed through the device of the recurrent hallucination, suggests an analogy between that part of Pip which wants Miss Havisham at least punished, at most removed from this earth for which she is so profoundly unfit, and the destroying fire itself.

CHRONOLOGY

1812

Charles Dickens born February 7 to John and Elizabeth Barrow Dickens.

1817

John Dickens transferred to Chatham.

1822

John Dickens transferred to London.

1824

Charles works at Warren's Blacking shoe polish factory; John Dickens imprisoned for debt at Marshalsea debtors' prison.

1824–1827

Attends Wellington House Academy.

1827

Works as office boy at law offices of Ellis and Blackmore.

1828

Learns shorthand, becomes court reporter.

1830

Gets reader's pass to British Museum; meets Maria Beadnell.

1832

Becomes parliamentary reporter.

1833

Publishes first sketch, "A Dinner at Poplar Walk"; organizes amateur theatrical productions.

1834

Continues to publish sketches; continues to work as newspaper reporter; breaks up with Maria Beadnell.

1836

Publishes *Sketches by Boz* in book form; begins *Pickwick Papers* (first novel) as monthly serial; marries Catherine Hogarth;

writes and produces *The Village Coquettes* and *The Strange Gentleman* (musical plays).

1837

Begins two-year stint as editor of *Bentley's Miscellany;* begins *Oliver Twist* (second novel) as monthly serial; birth of Charles Jr., first of Dickens's ten children; sister-in-law Mary Hogarth dies; writes and produces *Is She Your Wife?* (third musical play); completes *Pickwick Papers* and publishes in book form; Victoria becomes queen of England.

1838

Begins *Nicholas Nickleby* (third novel) as monthly serial; completes and publishes *Oliver Twist* in book form; birth of Mary, second child.

1839

Completes *Nicholas Nickleby* and publishes in book form; birth of Kate, third child.

1840

Publishes weekly magazine, *Master Humphrey's Clock;* begins *The Old Curiosity Shop* (fourth novel) as weekly serial.

1841

Completes and publishes *The Old Curiosity Shop* in book form; publishes *Barnaby Rudge* (fifth novel) as weekly serial, and then in book form; birth of Walter, fourth child.

1842

Visits North America for first time; publishes *American Notes* (first travel book); sister-in-law Georgina Hogarth joins Dickens household.

1843

Begins *Martin Chuzzlewit* (sixth novel) as monthly serial; publishes "A Christmas Carol" (story).

1844

Completes *Martin Chuzzlewit* and publishes in book form; travels with family to Italy; birth of Francis, fifth child; publishes "The Chimes" (second Christmas story).

1845

Edits the *Daily News* briefly; produces and acts in plays; birth of Alfred, sixth child; publishes "The Cricket on the Hearth" (third Christmas story).

1846

Publishes *Pictures from Italy* (second travel book); begins *Dombey and Son* (seventh novel) as monthly serial; publishes "The Battle of Life" (fourth Christmas story).

1847

Publishes "The Haunted Man" (fifth Christmas story); starts theatrical company and acts in benefit tour; birth of Sydney, seventh child; Emily Brontë writes *Wuthering Heights.*

1848

Completes and publishes *Dombey and Son* in book form; death of sister Fanny.

1849

Begins *David Copperfield* (eighth novel) as monthly serial; birth of Henry, eighth child.

1850

Founds his own weekly, *Household Words;* birth of Dora Annie, ninth child; Catherine suffers nervous breakdown, is replaced in household role by her sister Georgina; completes and publishes *David Copperfield* in book form; Nathaniel Hawthorne writes *The Scarlet Letter.*

1851

Death of father, John; death of daughter Dora Annie in infancy; begins *A Child's History of England* as monthly serial; Herman Melville writes *Moby-Dick.*

1852

Begins *Bleak House* (ninth novel) as monthly serial; publishes *A Child's History of England;* birth of Edward, tenth child.

1853

Completes and publishes *Bleak House* in book form; completes and publishes *A Child's History of England* in book form; gives benefit reading of "A Christmas Carol."

1854

Publishes *Hard Times* (tenth novel) as weekly serial and then in book form; Henry David Thoreau writes *Walden.*

1855

Begins *Little Dorrit* (eleventh novel) as monthly serial; Walt Whitman writes *Leaves of Grass.*

1856

Buys Gad's Hill Place.

1857

Completes and publishes *Little Dorrit* in book form; works on theatrical productions; meets actress Ellen Ternan.

1858

Separates from wife; gives public readings of his works; Abraham Lincoln, Republican candidate for U.S. Senate from Illinois, becomes famous as opponent of slavery in Lincoln-Douglas debates.

1859

Founds new weekly, *All the Year Round,* as a continuation of *Household Words;* publishes *A Tale of Two Cities* (twelfth novel) as weekly serial and then in book form.

1860

Publishes *The Uncommercial Traveller* (third travel book); begins *Great Expectation*s (thirteenth novel) as weekly serial; Lincoln elected president of the United States.

1861

Completes and publishes *Great Expectations* in book form; goes on tour giving public readings of his works; the Civil War breaks out in the United States.

1862

Victor Hugo writes *Les Misérables.*

1863

Death of mother, Elizabeth; Lincoln signs Emancipation Proclamation, delivers Gettysburg Address.

1864

Begins *Our Mutual Friend* (fourteenth novel) as monthly serial; death of son Walter, age twenty-two, of an aneurysm.

1865

Completes and publishes *Our Mutual Friend* in book form; publishes *The Uncommercial Traveller,* Volume 2 (fourth travel book); Leo Tolstoy writes *War and Peace;* President Lincoln is assassinated.

1866

Gives public reading tours; Fyodor Dostoyevsky writes *Crime and Punishment.*

1867–1868

Embarks on American reading tour (second visit to North America).

1869

Continues reading tours in England.

1870

Gives farewell reading in London; begins, but never finishes, *The Mystery of Edwin Drood* (fifteenth novel) as monthly serial; dies at Gad's Hill Place.

FOR FURTHER RESEARCH

ABOUT CHARLES DICKENS AND HIS WORKS

Peter Ackroyd, *Dickens*. New York: HarperCollins, 1990.

Monroe Engel, *The Maturity of Dickens*. Cambridge, MA: Harvard University Press, 1959.

George H. Ford, *Dickens and His Readers*. Princeton, NJ: Princeton University Press, 1955.

John Forster, *The Life of Charles Dickens*. 1874. Reprint, London: Dent, 1966.

Barbara Hardy, *The Moral Art of Dickens*. London: Oxford University Press, 1970.

Philip Hobsbaum, *A Reader's Guide to Charles Dickens*. London: Thames and Hudson, 1972.

Humphry House, *The Dickens World*. Oxford: Oxford University Press, 1941.

Thomas A. Jackson, *Charles Dickens, the Progress of a Radical*. New York: International Publishers, 1938.

Edgar Johnson, *Charles Dickens: His Tragedy and Triumph*. 2 vols. New York: Simon and Schuster, 1952.

Fred Kaplan, *Dickens: A Biography*. New York: William Morrow, 1988.

Wolf Mankowitz, *Dickens of London*. New York: Macmillan, 1976.

J. Hillis Miller, *Charles Dickens: The World of His Novels*. Cambridge, MA: Harvard University Press, 1958.

Claire Tomalin, *The Invisible Woman: The Story of Nelly Ternan and Charles Dickens*. New York: Knopf, 1991.

Angus Wilson, *The World of Charles Dickens*. New York: Viking Press, 1970.

ABOUT *GREAT EXPECTATIONS*

Nicola Bradbury, *Charles Dickens's* Great Expectations. New York: Simon and Schuster, 1990.

Janice Carlisle, ed., *Charles Dickens:* Great Expectations. New York: St. Martin's Press, 1996.

G.K. Chesterton, *Criticisms and Appreciations of Charles Dickens.* London: Dent, 1911, pp. 197–206.

H.H. Daleski, *Dickens and the Art of Analogy.* London: Faber and Faber, 1970, pp. 237–70.

Albert A. Dunn, "The Altered Endings of *Great Expectations:* A Note on Bibliography and First-Person Narrative," *Dickens Studies Newsletter* 9 (1978), pp. 40–42.

Charles R. Forker, "The Language of Hands in *Great Expectations,*" *Studies in Literature and Language* 3 (1961), pp. 280–93.

Joseph Gold, *Charles Dickens, Radical Moralist.* Minneapolis: University of Minnesota Press, 1972, pp. 241–54.

Bert G. Hornback, Great Expectations: *A Novel of Friendship.* Boston: Twayne, 1987.

John Lindberg, "Individual Conscience and Social Injustice in *Great Expectations,*" *College English* 23 (November 1961), pp. 118–22.

Thomas Loe, "Gothic Plot in *Great Expectations,*" *Dickens Quarterly* 6 (1989), pp. 102–10.

Carol Hanbery MacKay, "A Novel's Journey into Film: The Case of *David Lean's Great Expectations,*" *Literature Film Quarterly,* 13 (1985), pp. 126–34.

Brian McFarlane, "*David Lean's Great Expectations:* Meeting Two Challenges," *Literature Film Quarterly* 20 (1992), pp. 68–76.

Milton Milhauser, "*Great Expectations:* The Three Endings," *Dickens Studies Annual* 2 (1972), pp. 367–77.

Sylvere Monod, "*Great Expectations* a Hundred Years After," *Dickensian* 56 (September 1960), pp. 133–40.

Robert B. Partlow, "The Moving I: A Study of the Point of View in *Great Expectations,*" *College English* 23 (November 1961), pp. 122–26, 131.

Edgar Rosenberg, "A Preface to *Great Expectations,*" *Dickens Studies Annual* 2 (1972), pp. 294–335.

George Bernard Shaw, Introduction to *Great Expectations.* London: Limited Editions Club, 1937.

Ruth M. Vande Kieft, "Patterns of Communication in *Great Expectations,*" *Nineteenth-Century Fiction* 15 (March 1961), pp. 325–34.

Hana Wirth-Nesher, "The Literary Orphan as National Hero: Huck and Pip," *Dickens Studies Annual* 15 (1986), pp. 259–77.

George J. Worth, Great Expectations: *An Annotated Bibliography.* New York: Garland, 1987.

WORKS BY CHARLES DICKENS

Sketches by Boz (1836)

The Village Coquettes (1836), musical play

The Strange Gentleman (1836), musical play

Pickwick Papers (1836–1837)

Is She Your Wife? (1837), musical play

Oliver Twist (1837–1838)

Nicholas Nickleby (1838–1839)

The Old Curiosity Shop (1840–1841)

Barnaby Rudge (1841)

American Notes (1842), travel writing

"A Christmas Carol" (1843), short story

Martin Chuzzlewit (1843–1844)

"The Chimes" (1844), short story

"The Cricket on the Hearth" (1845), short story

Pictures from Italy (1846), travel writing

"The Battle of Life" (1846), short story

"The Haunted Man" (1847), short story

Dombey and Son (1846–1848)

David Copperfield (1849–1850)

A Child's History of England (1851–1853), nonfiction

Bleak House (1852–1853)

Hard Times (1854)

Little Dorrit (1855–1857)

A Tale of Two Cities (1859)

Great Expectations (1860–1861)

The Uncommercial Traveller (1861), travel writing

Our Mutual Friend (1864–1865)

The Uncommercial Traveller, Volume 2 (1865), travel writing

The Mystery of Edwin Drood (1870) (unfinished)

INDEX